# The Rustic Furniture Companion

# The Rustic Furniture Companion

## TRADITIONS, TECHNIQUES AND INSPIRATIONS

DANIEL MACK

**Lark Books**

Editor: Deborah Morgenthal

Art Director: Chris Colando

Library of Congress Cataloging-in-Publication Data
Mack, Daniel.

The rustic furniture companion: traditions,
techniques, and inspirations / Daniel Mack
p.   cm.
Includes index.
1. Furniture making.   2. Rustic woodwork.
3. Country furniture.
I. Title.
TT194.M23    1996
684.1'04--dc20                    95-40314
                                      CIP

ISBN 1-887374-65-5

10 9 8 7 6 5 4 3

Published in 1996 by Lark Books
50 College Street
Asheville, NC 28801

© Daniel Mack, 1996

Distributed in the U.S. by Sterling Publishing
  387 Park Avenue South, New York, NY 10016;
  1-800-367-9692
Distributed in Canada by Sterling Publishing
c/o Canadian Manda Group, One Atlantic Avenue,
  Suite 105, Toronto, Ontario, Canada M6K 3E7
Distributed in Great Britian and Europe by Cassell PLC, Wellington House,
  125 Strand, Londo, England WC2R 0BB
Distributed in Australia by Capricorn Link (Australia) Pty Ltd.,
  P.O. Box 6651, Baulkham Hills Business Centre, New South Wales 2153

Photos of contemporary furniture were contributed by the makers, except where noted. Most photos of Daniel Mack's work and projects are by Bobby Hansson; mantel, page 12, Lynne Reynolds; chair under stairs, page 21, N.O. Miller; locations pages 24–25, David Horton; forest photos, pages 8–9 and locations, pages 26–31, Daniel Mack. Other photo credits include: chest of drawers, Gustav Stickley's Craftsman Workshops (1899–1916), Eastwood and New York, NY, Los Angeles County Museum of Art, gift of Ellen and Max Palevsky, page 41; Charles Sumner's furniture, pages 42–43, Dan Gair; Ethiopian chairs, page 44, Douglas Dawson Gallery, Chicago; hedge chairs, page 46, and gypsy tables, page 47, Claudia Kinmonth; Windle Dill's Furniture, page 50, and woods, page 141, Richard Babb; rustic child's chair, page 130, Evan Bracken.

The furniture pieces in this book are the original creations of the contributing artists, who retain the copyrights to their individual designs.

Every reasonable effort was made to determine current copyright status for out-of-print books from which materials were excerpted. To the best of our knowledge they are in the public domain.

Every effort has been made to ensure that all the information in this book is accurate. However, due to differing conditions, tools, and individual skills, the publisher cannot be responsible for any injuries, losses, and other damages which may result from the use of the information in this book.

*Printed in Hong Kong*

### ACKNOWLEDGEMENTS

This book exists because of the generous cooperation of the many people whose lives are entwined with trees... rustic makers and their families.

I recognize my wife, Teri Mack, and a group of friends and colleagues who have made me smarter and more sensitive to the meaning of making objects: Bennett Bean, Darcy Brown, Bob Kushner, Mark Simon, Mahdad Saniee, and Elliot Zeisel.

My children, Kendra, Jessica, and Eliza Mack have supported me with their enthusiasm for both my tree work and my book work.

There are hundreds of clients who have given me the opportunity to develop my craft and art in the language of natural forms. I thank you.

Deborah Morgenthal and Rob Pulleyn at Lark Books have given me the support and encouragement to put words to the largely visual phenomenon of natural form furniture. They are well-skilled at their art.

# Contents

# Introduction

### BUILDING WITH NATURAL FORMS

This is my second book on rustic furniture from the point of view of the makers—the people who actually get the trees and use the tools and make the decisions about how it all goes together.

In recent years, the field has enjoyed renewed attention and there are a number of books on the market that cover the history and methods of making rustic furniture; my earlier book, *Making Rustic Furniture*, offers a fairly straightforward overview.

I've arranged these new materials as a scrapbook. A personally arranged collection of otherwise public information, a scrapbook tends to be slightly obsessive, with frequent leaps and lurches of rational thought. It's a perfect format for a book on rustic work: rustic objects are at once functional, ephemeral, and natural, and a nonlinear approach best suits the subject—and how I want to talk about it. In other words, the road I set us out on has a number of sudden detours and noteworthy side trips, but eventually, I deliver us in one piece to the desired destination. Where that is depends on your own expectations; it may mean you'll go right out and collect wood to make a chair, or, simply, that you'll appreciate a tree in a new way.

Those of us with the urge to build have usually favored beavers and birds, but a children's book, *Tenrec's Twigs* by Bert Kitchen (Philomel Press, 1990), helped broaden my views. It's about a groundhog, Tenrec, who finds himself the butt of jokes and comments from his fellow animals for his habit of building structures from sticks. He begins to doubt his avocation, until he visits The Milky Eagle Owl, who studies Tenrec's situation and then observes:

> *"Hmmm, I find your twig building very interesting, Tenrec. You seem very happy when you are building and you do not bother me, hmmm, or anyone else. In fact you may inspire others to build. My advice is to continue building!"*

*Above and opposite page: illustrations from* Tenrec's Twigs

# The Romance of the Tree

Rustic furniture evokes memories of the forest and the tree. These are very powerful, species-wide symbols with strong, but indistinct, personal meanings.

## HIDDEN MEANING

*Everything in this world has a hidden meaning... Men, animals, trees, stars, they are all hieroglyphics... When you see them, you do not understand them. You think they are really men, animals, trees, stars. It is only years later...that you understand.*

**Nikos Kazantzakis**

For thousands of years, the forest has been both a haven and a danger for humans, a place of solitude and loneliness, home to the sacred as well as the profane. The forest is a place of change, where the god turns demon and the prince becomes a beast. It is this very fusion of opposites within the forest that has riveted man's attention. Is the beautiful branch a snake? The fern, a spider?

In the midst of our ordered and "civilized" routines, the forest reminds us of the ongoing, dynamic forces of life—of the precarious illogic of living. The smells of a forest, the odors of fungus, mold, pollen, flesh—evi-

dence of decay and renewal—are both repulsive and invigorating, exciting and dreadful. Indeed, the forest is home to many of the rhythms and polarities of life: growth-death, expansion-contraction, inhale-exhale, danger-enchantment, the ordinary-the fabulous...the day, the month, the season.

The forest embodies both prehistory and the unknowable future. It exalts, delights, and feeds man with its beauty, and then reduces him to just another transient being dragging around his petty sack of fears and ambitions.

## FOCUSING ON THE TREE

Attention to the tree is a human way of making sense of the rich, dense overlay of forest life. The tree is a single, rooted, tall, and graceful survivor. In the tree, man finds a model and symbol of much of what he wants to know about life. The tree is generous with its shade, its wood, its oxygen, its bark, its fruit, its sap. The tree is a lesson in interdependence. We can "own" a piece of wood, but we share a tree.

All of this nuance and meaning get built into each rustic chair and table and bed. The history of the tree and the power of the forest are as much a part of rustic furniture as the joints and seating. Making, or owning, rustic furniture is a sign of recognizing the less than evident parts of life. It signifies a respect for the broken line of the natural world—the diverging branches that signify the constant forks and choices of life.

Changes of scale, proportion, and texture of rustic furniture indicate a willingness to endure primitive yet persisting feelings—small, helpless, safe, hidden, strong and many other feelings buried in our souls.

But the story of the forest is not the whole rustic story. There are eddies and variations as history weaves in and out of the trees. There are "styles" that creep into culture from nature, from the trees.

# The Romance of the Tree

### ECHOES OF THE PRIMITIVE

The most primitive style is the chair that merely reflects the use or mastery of natural materials in the service of man. This is primitive because it addresses a primary fear of the natural world. The chairs are fetishes, simple designs that indicate man can safely use natural materials. The implication is that the seemingly endless irregularity of nature can be enlisted in a regular, repetitive manner. It says there can be order from chaos.

# The Romance of the Tree

### CLASSICAL BEAUTY OF THE TREE CHAIR

There is a more intricate approach to tree furniture, built on the primitive foundation. This approach is more classical; with flourish and exuberance, the chairs become abstractions from nature, rejoicing in the variation and control of the organic form. They express a celebration of the unity with nature, not just the ability to coexist safely within it. There are formal elements and symmetries built into this approach to rustic furniture. These chairs often refer to other chairs, other styles and time periods. These chairs presuppose a knowledge of history.

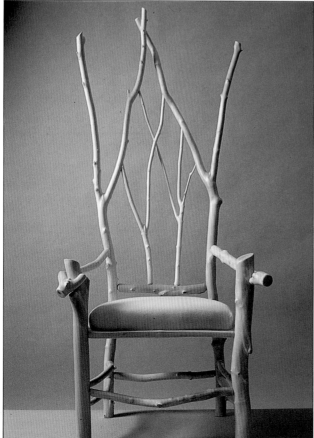

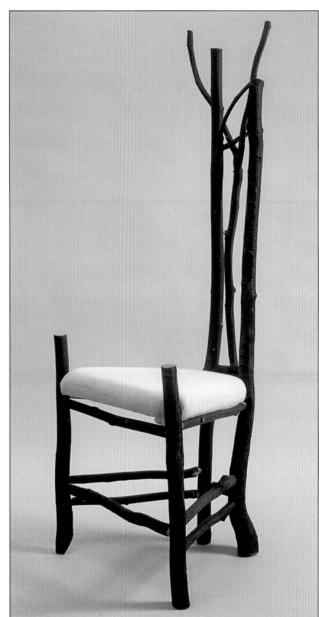

## THE EASTERN WAY

There is a third approach, an Eastern one. This one is not fearful in the face of nature like the primitive style, nor is it confident in its ability to transcend and control nature through knowledge or culture. The Oriental tradition, like the primitive, reflects awe for the forces of nature, and like the classical approach, it indicates that there is a larger system beyond the moment, but one beyond the knowledge or control of man. The chairs in this style are not merely tree concoctions, nor beautiful tree abstractions, but hybrid creatures, like the trees themselves. Rooted in the primitive earth and reaching gracefully to the sky, these chairs reflect the beauty of this relationship and the proportions of the space that separates them.

# The Romance of the Tree

### THE APPEAL OF TREE FORKS

My own work wanders through each of these traditions. I am basically a storyteller. I use three-dimensional objects to start a story and let the owner/user finish it. The "story" always starts in nature and the trees. One favorite "device" is the choice—the fork. Each of us is always at a fork: This way or that? Here or there? More or less?

14

I have always used this part of the tree. A fork requires and implies decisions about how big, how tall; it elevates or focuses the eyes. The crossed fork suggests that every choice is part of many more; no one fork is crucial.

I like the chance to get some of the majesty of the tree into my work. This is difficult because of the rescaling from the forest to the home. I keep trying.

# The Romance of the Tree

### MEMORY CHAIRS

My current work also ranges into history—the history of furniture, the history of mundane objects, and the history of chairmaking. I've come to call these Memory Chairs. They use common objects with strong natural forms to tell stories and evoke memories. These chairs evoke memories exactly because I use objects, both natural and made, that most people already have some experience with...fishing rods, hammers, boat oars... I'm working with an already stored bank of memories and associations.

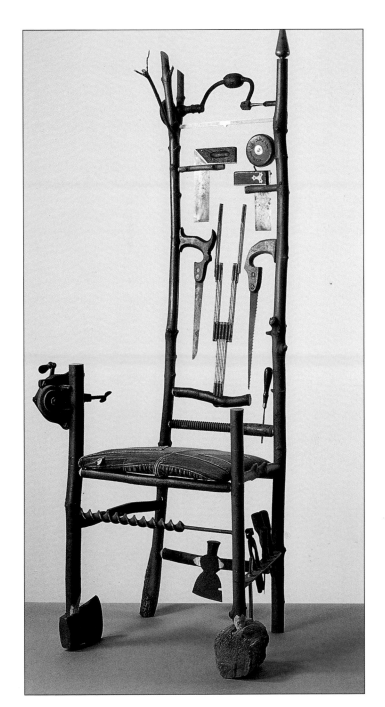

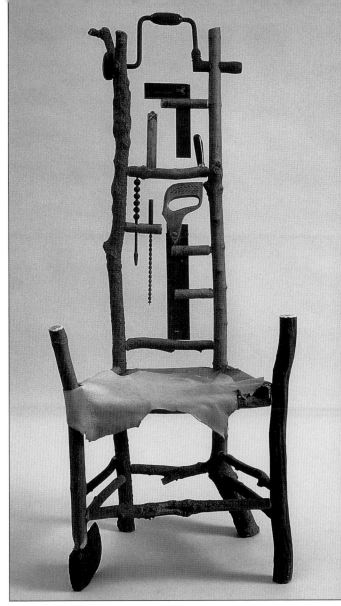

## TOOL CHAIRS

The Tool Chair series is a favorite of mine. There have been about ten so far, each with different emphatic characteristics: use of color, introduction of motion, and formal geometric shapes. They are as distinctive as siblings.

One important part of this series is repetition. As trees repeat, as tools are mass produced, so too the amalgam chairs echo this process. But the chairs also reflect the infinite variety of the trees and the different history of each tool as it has passed from user to user. Just as a tree is a tree and a tool is a tool, so too, no two trees are the same and no two tools ever get used in the same manner.

Another focus of this process is the use of common tools and common trees. A large part of the beauty of my natural-form work comes from the careful choice and combination of ordinary, almost forgettable, trees. It is similar with tools. I use everyday, almost culturally invisible tools; in

# The Romance of the Tree

their choice and placement, they take on beauty and transcendence. These chairs make a statement that beauty, grace, and harmony can be found in unexpected juxtapositions, in the tilted frame. And most importantly, making chairs in this way is not a unique event, a fortuitous accident. It can be done over and over. Each time is the same and different.

Certain aspects of the Tool Series have become signature elements. The use of a brace for a crown rail is, I think, a visually dynamic and successful way to define the top of a chair. It also allows me to pierce the tree and establish the intimacy of the work. The brace, designed to bore holes, retains its primitive function and goes on to get locked into the tree: It helps to define the negative space of the whole chair. There is a circular quality to this series. Like the snake swallowing its own tail, the chair has eaten the tools that made it. It implies a weary peace between man and nature.

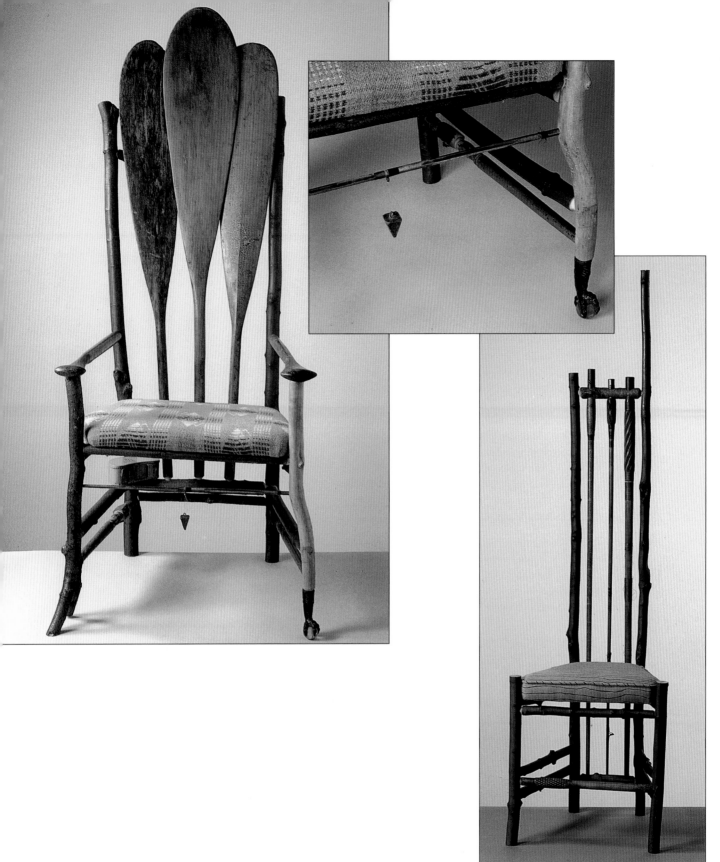

## SUMMER VACATIONS

Another aspect of this assemblage work is the opportunity to play with history and the passing of time. By including in my chairs antique tools and other old objects, I am showing respect for history and borrowing the meaning and longevity of these time-honored materials. I am working on a vacation series where objects from boating, sailing, fishing, and hunting are incorporated into chairs built, in part, with old porch furniture and driftwood. These chairs are meant to evoke the pleasant, purposeful, but not-too-serious nature of summer recreation.

# The Romance of the Tree

### NATURALLY PREUSED WOOD

Some of my natural-form work at this time centers on wood charged by history in a different way: The trees I use have been felled by beavers and then washed down the streams of the Catskills. The beavers will harvest almost every single tree in the area where they are building a dam. Those sharp little teeth ring and fell trees with the precision of an Eagle Scout's hatchet. Freshly felled trees have a sad, amazed quality. I often feel both surprise and anger at the beavers when I come across their work. But once the poles have spent a season or two in the water and have floated away and locked up in some log jam, they evoke a very different feeling. The little teeth marks are still there and the tips of the wood are still pointed, but nothing is sharp. The wood is now a gray-honey color and the nibbled ends invite examination. The wood has taken on an historical presence; its color and form tell the story of the beavers— and a larger story about the transformation of elements in nature.

When I collect this wood, I apply the same skills as I do with saplings: I look for interesting characteristics, correct proportions, and graceful curves. I choose wood in human-scale sizes—the diameter of an arm or a leg. The

chairs and beds that I make from this beaver-harvested wood seem to have emerged from the waters of a mountain river; they display the proud colors of the weather—the grays and leathery tans of forest survivors.

## PLACING A CHAIR

*Put a chair where you need to catch a newspaper, coat, purse, the mail, the keys, the cat. Watch the chair fill up, then empty it, and watch again.*

*Put a chair where it's unexpected; enjoy your surprise, this jolt of the new. Enjoy others as they discover it. Then enjoy knowing it's there and expecting to see it.*

*Acquire or commission a chair to commemorate an event. Make the chair part of a ritual. This world needs objects we charge with personal and collective meaning.*

*Put a chair where you want to remember something… the summer, the fall, a person, another place. Use the chair as a carriage into time.*

*Put a chair on a landing so that as you come up to it or walk down to it you can watch it change shape.*

*Put a chair in the strong light of a window or a spotlight.*

*Watch your chair grow shadows and throw them around.*

*Move chairs around.*

*Watch your friends and visitors react to your chairs. Who shares your humor? Your sense of beauty? Who gets invited back?*

# The Romance of the Tree

### RECONSTRUCTIONS, REPAIRS, AND AMENDMENTS

Another historically evocative approach is to combine parts of old or antique chairs with beautiful tree parts in order to create "fixed" chairs. The repair is neither authentic nor seamless, but reveals (and revels in) the distinctions in materials, joinery, and aesthetics. These become chairs from indistinct moments in time. They collapse the carefully constructed distinctions of time periods. All time is simultaneous: Is this a civilized chair turning primitive or a tree chair getting culture? From the family dump behind the barn, the trees seem to have unearthed discarded doorknobs, shelf brackets, and other decorative has-beens, and formed them into a tree chair that tells a story about a house.

## TOOLBOX CABINETS

To make cabinets, I use old toolboxes and mount them on legs from nature. The historical nature of the materials is immediately evident in the worn, useless toolboxes and the graceful legs from useless beaver-chewed trees. The cabinets comprise a strong, poetic opening to a story....about industrious, compulsive animals, men and their tools, the relentless passing of time, the importance of emptiness. The wear marks, the hasty repairs, the indistinct edges, the weathered paint, and the faint smells hint at the previous fullness and purpose. From this rich layered background, a simple new utility is suggested...a place to store keys, loose change, the day's mail, paper clips, safety pins, buttons, and all the other miscellaneous trinkets of daily life.

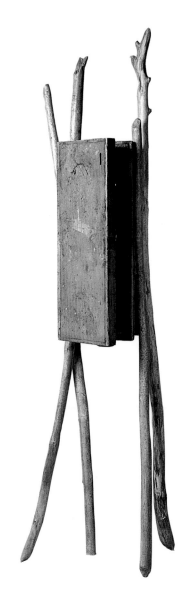

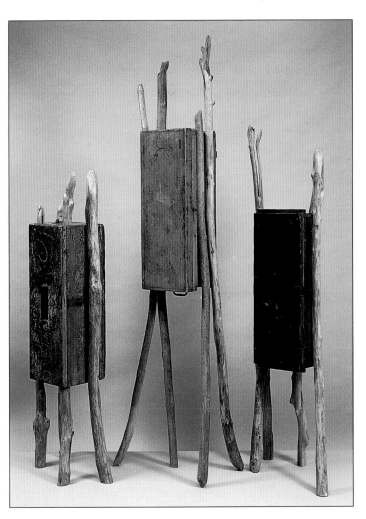

# The Romance of the Tree

### PLACEMENT AND PRESENTATION OF RUSTIC OBJECTS

*Tree chairs and other rustic furniture, because they are handmade and rooted in nature, are important objects in a home. The right place for a rustic chair is often immediately evident or nearly impossible to find.*

*Tree furniture defines places and events as important. It is frequently used to mark a commemoration, a ritual, or a tradition. I often give people rustic-handled silver spoons to celebrate a marriage, or a rustic child's chair to herald a first or second birthday. Many people like to incorporate signs of the natural tree world into marriage ceremonies, anniversaries, funerals, and other significant events.*

*I made the chair shown below in honor of Meryl Suzanne Weiss, who died of cancer at a young age. It marks the establishment of an endowed "Chair" of pediatric oncology at Children's Memorial Hospital in Chicago. I have also created a natural-form work for a room in an AIDS hospice. Again, the tree brings a degree of solace.*

*My chairs are often purchased to mark and celebrate a new home. They are placed on a landing, near the fireplace, in the entry, the bedroom...to complete a tableau and to continue a story about a particular family.*

*As the furniture maker, I begin the "story," but the day-to-day use of the object is its middle and end, which makes the placement and use of the furniture important. In Roman Europe, the word "family" included people, structures, land, animals, and furniture. A chair was part of the family and occupied a place in the family history. And as such, the chair provoked and evoked feelings.*

*All furniture stirs reactions in family and friends. There are encounters with furniture in the morning and at night. Furniture is a participant and a witness to the daily life of the household, part prop, talisman, icon, souvenir, badge....*

*The most common places for rustic furniture are the yard and the porch, where the story describes the*

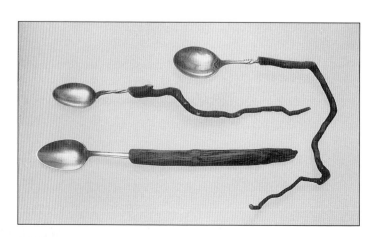

way casual, natural furniture marks the safe entry to the home. Nature has become friendly and inviting. The porch is also the traditional site of courting— the process that begins families.

Chairs and tables placed inside the house tell a slightly different story about juxtaposition and the cooperation of architecture and nature. Inside, the rustic reminds us about the source of architectural elements and the absence of true, straight lines in nature. Sometimes, rustic furniture may not start out with an overt purpose, but may take on an important function as it finds its place in the household. A rustic table or chair can serve to soften the straight, sharp edges of an architect's work, or offer consolation for an overscaled house. Rustic furniture may just become part of the family memory…"that chair in the den…." It also tends to function as the house jester, offering an unexpected, pleasant surprise and relief to the normal routine of daily life.

# Influences

**TRACING BACK** SOME OF THE INFLUENCES ON MY WORK IS LIKE TRYING TO REMEMBER ALL THE PARTS OF A DREAM: INVARIABLY, SOME PARTS ARE FORGOTTEN, OTHERS INVERTED, AND THE REST INVENTED. I'VE SPOKEN OF THE TREES AND THE FOREST AT GREAT LENGTH. I CAN MENTION, TOO, OTHER PERIODS, STYLES, AND MAKERS OF FURNITURE, BUT THERE ARE SCENES I'VE WITNESSED THAT ALSO HAVE LINGERING POWER.

SOMETIMES I GO TO THE WOODS, NOT WITH A SAW, BUT WITH A CAMERA. WHAT I CAPTURE IS THE FEELING I WANT TO PUT INTO A CHAIR. THIS FEELING RELATES TO SCALE, PROPORTION, TEXTURE, AMBIGUITY, TRANSITION, JUXTAPOSITION, AND TIME, AND IS BEST PUT INTO PIC- TURES. THESE SNAPSHOTS ARE VISUAL POEMS, AS GOOD RUSTIC FURNITURE SHOULD BE.

**THIS SCENE REFLECTS** THE PROMISE AND MYSTERY OF THE FOREST. THERE'S A WAY OUT, BUT IN BETWEEN IS THE LUSH DENSE FOREST FLOOR. WHAT'S AMONG THE FERNS? WHAT'S IN THE MURKY LIGHT?

**SOMETIMES I AM** SURPRISED BY
HOW TANGIBLE THE INFLUENCE OF
A PARTICULAR SCENE HAS BEEN.
THIS SCENE IN WESTERN IRELAND
IS ABOUT TIME, DECAY, MEMORIAL...
AND THE RELENTLESS REAPPEARANCE
OF SKY AND GRASS. THAT'S HOW I
WOULD DESCRIBE MY DRIFTWOOD
GHOST CHAIR.

# Influences

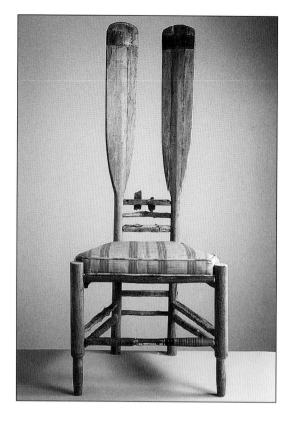

**AT MOHONK MOUNTAIN** IN NEW PALTZ, NEW YORK, IS THIS STILL A GRAND GAZEBO OR IS IT NOW AN OUT OF CONTROL TRELLIS? THE FEELING OF SOMETHING BEING TAKEN OVER IN EITHER FORM OR FUNCTION IS ALSO A PART OF MY RUSTIC WORK, AS SUGGESTED BY THE BLOCK ISLAND OAR CHAIR ABOVE.

**THIS STRUCTURE** SUGGESTS PROTECTION ON A BEACH, BUT THERE IS NO ROOF TO SHIELD THE SUN, NO SIDES TO STOP THE WIND, NO FLOOR TO STOP THE OCEAN. YET INSIDE IT FEELS LIKE PROTECTION. I CREATED A MUCH SAFER HAVEN IN THIS LIBRARY WITH A STRUCTURE AND A CHAIR THAT OWE A GREAT DEAL TO WHAT I OBSERVED ON THE BEACH.

THERE IS A SLIGHTLY OMINOUS QUALITY TO
THIS BEAUTIFUL OLD BENCH TUCKED INTO THE
UNDERCUT OF THIS ROCK. I LIKE THE BLENDING
OF THE COLORS AND TEXTURES. MY DRIFTWOOD
SETTEE TELLS A STORY ABOUT WILDNESS AND
USE...NOW AT REST ON BENIGN SHORES.

THE SUN PLAYS WITH THE METERED ORDER OF
A LADDER AND A SIMPLE STRUCTURE. THE
SHADOWS ADD AN EXTRA BEAUTY—POWERFUL,
BUT INSUBSTANTIAL. I AM OFTEN AWARE OF
THE SHADOWS CAPABLE OF BEING CAST FROM
MY CHAIRS.

# Influences

**THIS RED FENCE** IS A JOYOUS
SURPRISE: A DISCOVERY OF MAN
IN THE MIDST OF NATURE. THIS IS
THE PRESENCE OF THE JESTER. A
GOOD PIECE OF RUSTIC WORK
OFTEN PERFORMS A SIMILAR
SERVICE: A SMILE... THE PLEASURE
OF THE UNEXPECTED.

**THIS SCENE** AND THE FORKED CHAIR
BOTH SPEAK OF THE STARK FUSION OF
ORDER WITH NATURAL TEXTURE.

# Scrapbook History of Rustic Furniture

designs. These men were the tastemakers of the day, and their styles were copied and interpreted all over the woodworking world. The copying of existing designs marked a new self-consciousness about the use of the tree as a stylistic motif.

In fact, one of the trademarks of the Industrial Revolution was the use of mechanical inventions to create ever diverse styles of furniture. Some of these styles, such as the fanciful rustic, echoed an imaginary time when trees were chairs, and conveyed the evocative romance of the rustic. Not surprisingly, rustic life and handmade rustic objects grew more and more appealing as society became more urban and goods more mass produced; rustic represented a respite from, though not a reversal of, the locomotive of industrialization.

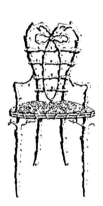

If it is true that there were trees before there were people, then the roots of rustic furniture predate man's memory. This leaf fossil from a sycamore-family tree is from the time of the dinosaurs. It's helpful and humbling to be reminded that the makings of rustic work have been around longer than we have and may possibly outlive us all. And that is a big part of the magnetism of the rustic. That tree, those forests have a soothing, long-lived magic...and that is what gets built into each and every chair.

History is full of references to the rustic. It was the Tree of Knowledge that started history, and ever since, trees have been used in the service of society: to frame huts and houses, to form tables, doors, gates, and seats. But it wasn't until the mid-18th century that rustic furniture as we know it now first emerged.

At the same time, designers such as Thomas Chippendale and Matthew Darly were publishing books of fashionable furniture

*Opposite page and below: fanciful rustic chairs from the mid 1700's*

and spiritual fibers of society. Rustic was viewed as one kind of material antidote to the ills created by the interiority of the city, indeed of civilization itself.

J.J. Thomas, author of *Rural Affairs* (Albany, New York: Luther Tucker & Son, 1858), encouraged an attention to the shapes and textures of nature and an engagement with doing and making. His illustrations of rustic seats and structures have the same feel as the drawings a century earlier (see Darly drawing below). There are really no directions for making this furniture and the designs seem to spring from a pen rather than from actual trees. Nonetheless, the designs shown on the following pages mark the spirit that carries through to rustic work today.

Throughout the 19th century, as industrialization continued to change the face and pace of the world, there were reactions that addressed the need for connection to the vanishing past. In the 1840s and 1850s, the Grimm brothers were collecting old folktales. Transcendentalism, a philosophy that asserted the primacy of the spiritual over the material world, was just forming. In England, John Ruskin was championing the humanizing of industry, and William Morris was articulating in word and deed the ideals of a return to the integrity of hand work in the face of the machine. In America, Walt Whitman, Henry David Thoreau, and Ralph Waldo Emerson were actively espousing the need to integrate the natural world into one's daily life.

It was a time when the seers of the age, the poets and philosophers, novelists and essayists, were trying to make sense of the impact of the Industrial Revolution on the physical

# Scrapbook History of Rustic Furniture

Rural Affairs *by J.J. Thomas, 1858, from which "Rustic Seat and Structures" is excerpted*

## RUSTIC SEATS AND STRUCTURES

*A great reform is needed among country residents in relation to the attractions for open air. There are members of every family who suffer serious loss both in health and spirits, from an almost perpetual confinement within doors. Trees, flowers, walks, and shady seats, are far more important than splendid drawing rooms and costly furniture. The most pleasant and agreeable summer parlor the writer ever occupied, and in which he has spend many days during the heat of summer, was formed only by the dense shade of leafy boughs overhead, beneath which the cooling breezes could freely pass among the trunks of the trees. For the purpose of inviting attention to the increase of these out-of-doors attractions, by pointing out a mode of providing such summer parlors as these with the appropriate furniture within the reach of all, and for adding to the interest of more secluded parts of the ornamental grounds, we propose to devote a short chapter.*

*Seats, arbors, and other structures, made of rustic work, that is, of the trunks and branches of trees in their natural forms, have much to commend them to the peculiar wants of landscape gardening in America. They admit a great display of taste and ingenuity, with but little cost—an important consideration where the motto of the people must be, "profuse of genius, not profuse with gold."*

*Figure 1*

*Figure 2*

*Figure 3*

*There are very few of our countrymen who will consent to give a highly polished air to their grounds, except in the immediate proximity to their dwellings, and even here the claim to much finish, is commonly a very doubtful one at best. It is even rare to find other parts of ornamental grounds so highly kept, that such costly ornaments as vases and statues are not quite out of place; and it is quite as rare to find those who ought to be so lavish of their money as to incur the expense.*

*Most objectionable of all, on the score of taste, are those heavy wooden structures, made of elaborate carpentry, for the support of climbing plants, or for summer shelter, so commonly seen in various parts of the country. Nothing can be more incongruous than the forces connexion between those most delicate and graceful of all plants, twiners and*

*Figure 4*

climbers, and stiff, formal and heavy board supports. A simple and appropriate rustic material is as much superior to these, as a charcoal sketch by a skillful artist, is superior to the rich daubings of a sign painter.

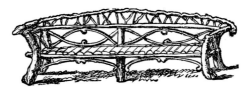

Figure 5

It should be distinctly remembered, however, that rustic structures should not be placed near a highly finished dwelling, but in the less formal and more sequestered parts of the grounds, except it be those of a smaller size, and of the more simpler forms. On the other hand, a small cottage, possessing little formality, will more freely admit these structures in all situations.

Figure 6

In order to succeed in constructing rustic work, the first thing is to procure the materials. All such objects as may be exposed to the weathers should be of the most durable wood, of which red cedar is the best. For certain purposes, white oak will answer well, but as it is essential to have the bark remain on, the wood should be cut at a time of year when this will not peel or separate. If cut towards the close of summer, the wood will last about twice as long as when cut in winter or spring. A horse load or two, of boughs or branches of trees, of which a goodly portion may be curved and twisted, from one to six inches in diameter, will constitute the materials for a good beginning.

Among the simplest objects, are rustic stools, figs. 1 and 2, which nearly explain themselves. The first is made of nearly straight pieces, put together by boring holes for the principal framework, and using nails for the smaller pieces. The second is simpler and stronger, but requires two curved branches or portions of roots. The rustic chair, fig. 3, has the face of the back and seat made of "wood mosaic," a mode of facing flat surfaces of boards and plank

Figure 7

Figure 8

represented more distinctly by figs. 9 and 10,—the small and straight shoots which are split into two parts for this purpose, being, unlike other rustic material, with smooth back. This mode of working admits of the exercise of much taste and ingenuity, as rods having differently colored bark may be used and so arranged as to give an interesting variegated appearance. This kind of work, is often used with great advantage for facing the interior walls of rustic summer houses; and in all cases, the

*Figure 9*

*Figure 10*

design, however simple, should be first marked with chalk on the board-facing intended to be covered. It is usually made of the halved rods as shown in fig. 9; but for the bottoms of seats, a more even surface is presented by shaving the edges, as in fig. 10. Sometimes bark alone is used for this purpose.

Fig. 4 is a lighter and simpler chair. The outer portion of the back will be strongest if in one piece, and a portion of wild grape-vine may be advantageously employed. The seats shown in figs. 5 and 6 require but little explanation. Fig. 5 may be formed of nearly straight pieces of wood; the back of fig. 6 will require 2 or 3 crooked pieces strongly and neatly spliced together. It may be well to add here, that the perfection of all rustic work renders very close and perfect joints absolutely necessary. The back of the seat shown by fig. 7 is let into or fastened to the middle of the tree.

The table, fig. 8, is formed of the trunk of a tree with well selected branches, inverted; to the top of which is nailed circular boards, battened crosswise together, and covered with "wood mosaic" already described.

*Figure 12*

*Figure 11*

Fig. 11 is a flower stand, supported by a leg formed of the branching trunk of a tree, with braces nailed on below. The top is wicker-work and will receive a round tin pan, filled with clear wet sand, and covered with a lid of basket or sieve-work, through the openings in which the stems of flowers may be thrust into the sand, which will keep them fresh for several days. Fig. 12 is a similar stand, made stronger, to hold a box or pot of rooted plants.

Fig. 13 is a pedestal for flower-pots, and may be a neat and handsome ornament for any part of the grounds. It is easily made of a wooden box, covered with the mosaic of wood.

Fig. 14 is a rustic arbor, requiring but little explanation. If the straw forming the thatched roof, is kyanized, it will last a long time. The cornice is ornamented with cones of the white pine, nailed to the horizontal board supporting the roof. Cones of different size are very suitable for interior cornices of rustic buildings....

Fig. 15 ... (is also a) rustic arbor, with variations in design.

All the structures we have described, taken together, if built in the best manner, would not cost so

*Figure 13*

*Figure 14*

*Figure 15*

*much as single statues or vases of marble; and as proof of their durability when made of the right materials, we may state that there are specimens in England, which have been exposed to all weathers, now more than forty years old.*

# Scrapbook History of Rustic Furniture

## ARTS AND CRAFTS IN AMERICA 1875-1920

As a maker and designer of rustic furniture for the last 15 years, I am drawn to the beautiful, quiet, broken line of the tree and the branch. But I have seen my eye equally drawn to the objects and philosophy of the Arts and Crafts movement—perhaps one of the most prominent and long-lived responses to the Industrial Revolution. It has taken me a while to see the

parallel and intersecting themes in both these areas of decorative arts. There are also striking parallels between these arts at the end of the last century and the end of this present one.

The main tenet of the Arts and Crafts philosophy was that a healthy society is possible only if the individual feels respected, has some degree of control in his life, and has the opportunity to experience nature and beauty. John Ruskin enchanted many minds and hearts of a generation with his words: "Life without industry is guilt; industry without art is brutality."

The idealistic thrust of this movement was to create a new industrialism that fused the power of art into the strength of labor. In this process, many believed that the needed social reforms of the period could then be addressed. Beautiful objects were to be the end result of contented labor. This movement was a mix of social conscience, optimism, fear of runaway industrial capitalism, and nostalgia for distant times no one really remembered.

The philosophy was not antimachine; rather, it emphasized using the machine to produce quality goods at affordable prices. Work was to be a joyous combination of the hand and heart of the worker and the use of the machine. This was the "mission" and the name Arts and Crafts furniture came to be called.

Gustav Stickley, the leading promoter of Arts and Crafts in the United States, believed that Americans needed to learn a new sense of taste based on natural beauty, rather than cost, and a new way of putting materials together to

create simple, individualized, and dignified objects. He founded a new factory called United Crafts to make furniture based on these principles. He also set about teaching the public how to live the Arts and Crafts philosophy with the publication of The Craftsman, a monthly magazine that he launched in 1901. The magazine featured articles about how to furnish a home, plant a garden, appreciate Native-American music, explore the natural world, and much more. In the following essay, Stickley addresses how to appreciate the wood that is used for making household furniture.

The tangible implications of the philosophy were reflected in architecture, furniture, lighting, textiles, and tabletop accessories. Objects were to reflect a respect for the materials they were made from. Lamps were made from plain wood, hammered copper, and iron; textiles were made from straight linen panels with embroidered designs of nature motifs. And of great importance was that architecture and objects reflect a sense of regionality—a slippery notion now that goods from one region were being distributed across the country.

Stylistically, the furniture of the Arts and Crafts movement echoed the scale and line of what was thought to be medieval—simple and sturdy, with hewn lines. In reaction to the dense, dizzying decoration of contemporary Victorian furniture, ornamentation was to be minimal. Wood was celebrated for its graining and was used in straight lengths, often milled in an extravagant quarter-sawn pattern, worked, and machined. There was a strong vein of traditionalism within Arts and Crafts that tapped preindustrial and primitive longings. The furniture and accessories became props for a subtle escapism from the nasty, metastasizing industrialization of the era.

The message was clear: At least in the home, you can purchase or make objects that address the part of your spirit that is assaulted by the world, confused by the pace of production, and weary of consumption. Part of the "sell" of Arts and Crafts was the appeal of another time when things were simpler,

## "THE VALUE OF A RIGHT APPRECIATION OF WOOD"
### by Gustav Stickley

*A well-known writer on Japanese architecture and interior decoration says: "To the Japanese, wood, like anything that possesses beauty, is almost sacred, and he handles it with a fineness of feeling that at best we only reveal when we are dealing with precious marbles. From all wood that may be seen close at hand, except such as is used as a basis for the rare and precious lacquer, paint, stain, varnish, anything that may obscure the beauty of texture and grain, is rigidly kept away. The original cost of the material is a matter of no consequence; if it has a subtle color, a delicate swirl in the veining, a peculiarly soft and velvety texture, it is carefully treasured and used in the place of honor."*

*We of the Western world are as yet only beginning to appreciate what this may mean. With us, the original cost of the material is a matter of the greatest possible consequence, and we are too apt, when we are choosing wood for the interior of our houses or for the making of our furniture, to put a money value upon it rather than*

*Stickley-style rustic chair, Daniel Mack*

*to allow ourselves to appreciate its natural beauty. For it is a fact that the greatest beauty often lies in wood that is faulty and comparatively valueless from a commercial point of view, and that by throwing this aside we sacrifice the most interesting characteristic of the woodwork. When we do strive for the effects produced by crooked growth and irregular grain, we go to the other extreme and instead of studying each particular piece of wood and using it exactly where it belongs with relation to the rest, we hunt out deliberately the most gnarled and knotted pieces, so that the result instead of being interesting in a natural and inevitable way, is eccentric and artificial.*

*This is the greater pity because, after all, it requires only a little interest, care and discrimination to give to the woodwork of a room just the kind of interest and beauty that belong to it. Instead of that we are apt either to imitate the wealthy man who built a cottage in the Adirondacks and paneled it throughout with spruce so carefully selected that not a single knot appeared throughout the entire house, or else we go to the opposite extreme and deliberately select the wood of irregular and faulty grain for the entire house, instead of letting it appear here and there as is natural.*

■

# Scrapbook History of Rustic Furniture

more honest. (This sounds remarkably like the credo of the 1960s and, in a quieter way, of the views of a growing number of people at the end of this century.)

## RUSTIC FURNITURE ENLISTED IN THE SERVICE OF ARTS AND CRAFTS

The dominant form of rustic furniture found in the Arts and Crafts movement was a manufactured style. The biggest producer was a factory, the Old Hickory Furniture Company of Shelbyville, Indiana. The factory actually grew and harvested straight young hickory trees to be bent in forms to exact, determined shapes. Similarly, all the joints were machine-cut mortise and tenons which were nailed through. This furniture was the first successful application of manufacturing factory techniques to the heretofore erratic, eccentric, home-based world of rustic furniture. The "style" of Old Hickory and its several competitors was the use of straight lines. This meant clear, straight saplings. There were no burls, forks, galls, or other oddities of real trees. The "natural" quality of the product was that the bark was left on the wood. Otherwise, it was handled and finished like any other manufactured chair.

The point is that straight stock is easiest to tend, harvest, to transport, to store, manipulate, and machine. In other words, it makes dollars and cents to use the most homogenized trees possible for a manufactured product. The manufacturing process dictates the straight stick style—not the natural forms of the trees nor the individual design ideas of the workers.

This manufactured rustic style was predictable or standardized, affordable, and available. Every chair looked exactly like the one in the catalog or the drawing in the magazine. It allowed for the philosophical and technical architects of the Arts and Crafts movement to retain design influence of what the correct "look" was. That look included the primitive, nature-based furniture from simple, direct, honest materials. It spoke about the strong individual who was tied through rustic work and Arts and Crafts life to the traditions of early America, the guilds of medieval times, and the lost integrity of the Native Americans. The citizen was encouraged to do it. Or if that was not possible, he could buy into it. Never was the Arts and Crafts movement truly very far from the center of the industrial capitalism it railed against; basically, the style of rustic furniture it promoted was factory-made.

## REEMERGENCE OF ARTS AND CRAFTS AND RUSTIC

In the early 1970s, both Arts and Crafts and rustic styles resurfaced as uncomplicated alternatives to years of modernist and art furniture. The current draw of Arts and Crafts is very similar to its original magnetism: It has bold, distinct, unadorned lines that reveal the materials and the joinery. Now there is a double echo of history. The harking back is to preWar America, rather than to medieval furniture or Native Americans or guilds. The problem is that the prices of the original Arts and Crafts objects have hit, and hovered in, the realm of the collectors. This has spawned a growing number of reproducers and interpreters who sell their work in custom shops and mail-order catalogs. For different price points, almost any consumer can now buy into the Mission look; moreover, there are plans available in woodworking magazines for the home builder.

Rustic furniture has a related, but slightly different story. One constant tap root of this style has been people who we would now refer to as "off the grid." These were people who were loosely tied to the mainstream economy; they had the character and need to tinker. Sometimes the paths of these people crossed the main road and they were "discovered," but that was never the primary goal. They were driven by some personal or family or religious conviction that kept them at an arms distance from the shopping mall.

The original Arts and Crafts movement attracted similar characters for whom an alternative lifestyle was more important than the objects of their work. More than 4,000 people wrote to me after my article on rustic work appeared in *The Mother Earth New*s in 1987. Not one person was a "customer." They were interested in doing it.

Similarly, the explosive popularity of log homes and the country look has fuelled the taste for affordable rustic furniture. Log home dwellers and country-look decorators are very busy marketing a look of honest simplicity in the face of ever-more electronic interconnection. Can a Rustic Fair on the Shopping Channels be very far off?

## DIFFERENCES BETWEEN ARTS AND CRAFTS AND RUSTIC

Rustic has always been fundamentally democratic whereas the Arts and Crafts movement has had tiers of members. With simple tools and ubiquitous materials, anyone can make a rustic chair and put a "for sale" sign on it in the front yard. Arts and Crafts designs are more complicated to make and sell. Rustic work is a haven for souls who are, to some degree, twisted in body and mind by industrial capitalism. Men and women have gone to the woods and remade themselves as rustics after leaving corporations, the military, the media, the assembly line, and other manual labor work where their bodies wore out. There is a vital, reclusive quality to rustic work that was often just an elusive ideal for the original Arts and Crafts reformers.

This element of rugged individualism is the core attraction for consumers of rustic work. With each chair, they get evidence that some individual had the time and spirit to actually make this. They are buying a piece of the optimism of the makers.

On the other hand, even today, the most "successful" rustic makers are those who have adopted some consumer conventions in the production and marketing of their work. Efficient production requires the pyramidal division of labor with a large, modestly paid labor pool, usually called subcontractors, on

*Chest of Drawers, 1912–1916, detail, Gustav Stickley's Craftsman Workshops*

the bottom; it requires a promotional plan that allows customers to get what they have seen in a catalog, and a marketing system that allows for one or two markups before the product gets to the user. This may mean craft shows, trade shows, a "rep," a showroom, a store or gallery…Entrepreneurial rustics have to behave primarily like entrepreneurs.

The rustic idiom—the celebration of natural forms as part of utilitarian objects—appears in contemporary European furniture and in modern sculpture. And there is an exploding business in Malaysia and China making rustic objects for export to the United States. Catalogs are full of rustic everything. Rustic may be more like a building block of style than a period or style.

In summary, the Arts and Crafts movement was an available dream vehicle for America. It offered a relief, a "new" look with comforting references to the past, and a stylistic distinction between generations of furniture buyers. The movement was a marketing vehicle for designers and producers. It was a central theme for dozens of small- and medium-size entrepreneurs who were able to successfully fuse innovation, ambition, and the draw of the hand-crafted alternative. The Arts and Crafts philosophy worked for 15 or 20 years and it is working again. Then as now, rustic furniture provided a strong supporting role. But in between, rustic furniture has had its own separate history.

# Scrapbook History of Rustic Furniture

### PROFILE: CHARLES SUMNER (1856-1939)

One important artist of the Arts and Crafts time period, whose work is enjoying renewed favor, was Charles Sumner. Rustic dealer Bert Savage, owner of Larch Lodge in Center Stafford, New Hampshire, has collected information on this builder of rustic work who was active in rural Maine during the early years of the 20th century, and wrote the following profile about his life and work.

*The furniture of Charles Sumner relied heavily on mosaic twig veneer worked into fanciful and unique designs. He lived for 83 years, his known furniture production occurred only during the 1920s. As with other rustic makers of this period, Sumner produced pieces as a part-time business and to pass the time during the harsh northern winters.*

*Born to farming parents in Leeds, Maine, Sumner was running the family farm by age 20. By 1887, he had moved to Lewiston, Maine, then a city with a population of 20,000. His listed occupations there were "laborer" and "teamster." In 1899, then married, he moved to Mexico, Maine, where he worked in similar jobs. He stayed in that town until his wife's death in 1919. Nothing in the written record indicates that at age 64 he was about to start making important rustic furniture.*

*During the 1920s, he worked as a caretaker at the Birch Point Camps owned by John L. Howard. It is there that he made most of his twig furniture. These*

*sporting camps, located on the edge of the western Maine wilderness, afforded Sumner an abundance of raw materials; populated by sportsmen, the camps provided him with customers. In 1929, John Howard sold the camps, perhaps ending Sumner's stay there. Until his death in 1939, he maintained a legal residence at his niece's home in Lewiston, Maine, where he also may have made furniture.*

*Of the 21 pieces of furniture that can now be attributed to Sumner, there are five front desks, 12 tables or stands, a settee, a swivel desk chair, and a book shelf. The mosaic designs that cover the pieces are unique. There are stars, circles, chevrons, swirls, octagons, diamonds, ovals, rectangles, and squares. Two tables have written inscriptions worked with twigs. One includes the word "souvenir" in an obvious bit of commercialism.*

*It is the selection of woods and the final designs that make Sumner's work so fascinating. The exterior wood he used most often appears to be northern arrowwood, with striped maple used occasionally to add texture. There are contemporary references to his having used these woods, whose special properties made*

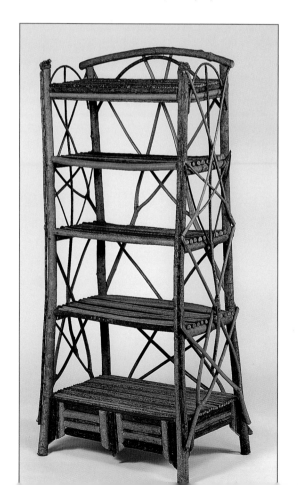

them successful veneer material. Arrowwood has very straight branches; the name derives from the fact that Native Americans are reported to have used it to make arrow shafts. The color of its bark can vary a great deal, from yellow to red, or an interesting mottled combination of the two. Arrowwood forms near perfect two or three twig forks, which Sumner used to embellish all his known pieces. The use of arrowwood forks can almost be considered his signature. The wood used for the finishing touches, finials, and drawer handles, are often wonderful pieces of burl.

To construct the mosaic veneer that is nailed down, he first split most of the twigs in varying degrees to adjust their diameter to create a flat surface when assembled. There is no indication that Sumner first drew a pattern directly on the frame of the piece.

Sumner was an avid recycler. This was no doubt more from economic necessity than from a spirit of conservation. He built the hidden structure from recycled cardboard and wooden shipping crates, parts of old furniture, buildings, and docks. Interesting labels and inscriptions appear on the recycled parts. Nails seem to be the only item that he had to buy to make this furniture.

Drawers were certainly a favorite design element, and he worked them in wherever he could. Desks have up to eight drawers, including the usual two interior ones. Tables and stands have drawers concealed by their elaborate aprons. Drawers are of nailed constructions, with the larger ones having side runners.

One can only guess at the inspiration for his twig work. Sophisticated mosaic work was being done in the central Adirondack area of New York in the late 19th century for the great camps that were being constructed at that time, but it is hard to imagine him having had an opportunity to see that work.

Sumner's total production will probably never be known. His known work has descended through relatives or from the Birch Point Camps. It is likely that much of it was destroyed by fire, weather, or neglect. His obituary made no mention of his twig work; apparently it was not considered important at the time. Today, 56 years later, his talent has been rediscovered and he is viewed as a truly outstanding rustic furniture maker and American folk artist.

*Charles Sumner's work, 1924–1928; profile written by Bert Savage*

43

# Scrapbook History of Rustic Furniture

Ethiopian wooden chairs, Douglas Dawson Gallery, Chicago

## INTERNATIONAL ROOTS

Given the universal distribution of trees and the ever-present human ingenuity, it would seem that some form of "rustic" furniture could be found all over the world. A number of examples of international rustic have crossed my path in the last few years.

### Ethiopia

Here are two examples of 19th-century chairs from Ethiopia. Called *gurage*, each is carved from one large piece of wood. The single large trunk of wood is treated more as a carving material than as a tree being celebrated, and ends up in a formal, yet beautiful shape.

### Guatemala

Michael Armstrong of Paonia, Colorado, learned to make the stool shown below while in Guatemala.

## Britain

Much of the rustic furniture as we know it has ties to Britain and to English garden furniture. Here are some drawings from a 1912 garden catalog from The Cooper Company in London.

## Ireland

I taught a workshop in Western Ireland a few years ago. No one claimed to ever have heard of rustic furniture, and the idea of furniture made from raw tree parts was considered laughable. But in just a few days, the dozen students had not only caught onto the techniques of rustic building, but had gone out and scavenged wood for their own designs.

*(Thanks to the Margaret Woodbury Strong Museum in Rochester, NY)*

*Students at the Furniture College in Letterfrack, Connemara, Ireland, above and on page 46*

# Scrapbook History of Rustic Furniture

There was one important exception. Two students saw some scrubby saplings recently cut in the row between two fields, near a road. They asked the farmer if they could have the few trees, and he very firmly said no, he had use for that wood. I was struck by the stingy nature of his response. Coming as I did from America, where "brush" can mean trees up to four feet in diameter, people are always paying somebody to take away their trees. That's not the case in Ireland. Trees are a political issue. I was told of the wholesale logging of the island by Cromwell. The event was described with such energy that I had to work hard to remember that Cromwell died in 1540. I began to see that I didn't understand very much about trees in Ireland.

After teaching this workshop, I became very interested in Irish vernacular furniture and read any books I could get on the subject, hoping to see a branch or two sticking out of a cottage corner. Of great help was *Irish Cottage Furniture*, by Claudia Kinmonth (Yale University Press, 1992).

*Left:* Hedge chairs, Irish Cottage Furniture, *page 29*

As a result of my reading, I learned a great deal about the bottomless ingenuity of the Irish. From the crucible of poverty came the habits of what we would call "recycling." In the coastal areas, shipwrecks provided a regular supply of unusual salvage, and much of the furniture in coastal towns bears the mark of reused shipping cartons and wood from wrecked boats.

Similarly and of more interest to me, was the use of "hedge wood"—that scrubby, gnarled thicket that grows between fields. As far back as the start of the 19th century, there are references to "hedge carpenters," the lowest paid of the wood craftsmen. It was their talent to find and "see" parts of chairs already grown in the twisted hedges.

From necessity or disposition, hedge carpenters were not vexed by the need for milled lumber with its straight edges; hedge wood, in a poor country, had value. It was used for fencing, gates, garden stakes, and kindling, as well as chair and table parts. I thought again about the reluctant farmer and his cut saplings, and wasn't quite so judgmental.

Hedge chairs look regular if you squint at them. They look like what I call Captain's Chairs; each has a low back with spindles set into the plank seat and the curved crown rail. This curved crown rail is a found curved piece of wood. These chairs seem related to the Windsor chairs; there is an ongoing tradition of such country "stick" chairs in England, where they are called Falls Chairs; there are also examples of these chairs in Australia, where the Irish often migrated.

My theory, at the moment, is that the perceptual and technical skills of the Irish hedge carpenters made their way to the United States, Canada, and Australia in the successive waves of Irish immigrations throughout the 19th century and formed one strong tap root of the rustic tradition.

The chair, (on right) recently made by William McCardle in Tyler, Texas, is in direct line of the Hedge Chairs, pictured in the Kinmonth book (shown here on page 46, below left).

Kinmonth has the picture below of a gypsy table in her book. Anyone with the least knowledge of American rustic will recognize this. Did it come from Ireland, or is it such a universal form that it just sprang up everywhere?

(A variation of this table is described in the projects section on page 124.)

# Gallery of Contemporary Rustic Furniture Makers

In my 15 years in this field, I've seen the tides of business swell and the magazines exalt and celebrate us neo-primitives. I've seen some of my rustic colleagues develop into entrepreneurs and some entrepreneurs flourish as rustics. Behind all this activity is the charm of the trees. The magazine writers and curators recognize that charm: It's like the sun bouncing off a little bit of quartz rock—a common, everyday dazzle like great shadows—ordinary and awesome at once.

Beyond the public hoopla about rustic traditions and revivals is an ever-growing number of people attracted by the rustic and its promises. They are not all marbles-in-the-mouth country carpenters who whack sticks together in some remote barn. Some tell of a journey from the city to the forest and back again. Taken together, the letters, the brochures, and conversations create a body of semireligious references to a personal if not an actual journey...through many jobs, companies...ending up in the ephemeral world of tree furniture. Most of them stay where they are and who they are: a fireman in Jersey City, an arts administrator, a bottled-water salesmen, a housebound mother or father.

In the rustic they see and experience the thrill of the act of making something. That act is an exercise in hope, a tonic for despair. Most of the rustic people I know are optimists. They believe in the future—that it will treat them well. They make beautiful, unusual objects that usually no one has requested. Like other artists, they are taking a leap of faith and making a statement about themselves and their relationship to the larger world.

Rustic makers encounter the passing of time in a new way. First they must find the time to learn a bit about the field, then the time to acquire the materials and the few tools required, and finally the time to assemble something. All along they are confronting their own rhythms—their insecurity at finding tools and materials, their impatience at drying the materials, and the frustration of finding storage and work space. Then there is the crusty delight of actually making a particular piece of work from all these hard-earned sticks... what if...it doesn't work out...

For some, rustic work is really just busy work while they spend time with themselves. This is part of the spiritual and poetic element of rustic building: After a visit to the woods to gather branches, the maker emerges to make something, and in that process she remakes and rebuilds a part of herself.

For all of us at times, rustic work is really a job, a way to make money and raise a family. Many have come to it from other manual trades and crafts after disillusion, accidents, or worn muscles. For many, including myself, it has been a significant way to learn about manual work. I spent most of my life in and around the head trades—journalism and college teaching—which had the effect of creating a barrier between me and handwork. Rustic work was an inviting way into the satisfaction of making something.

## ORGANIZATION OF THE GALLERY

I tried at first to organize the current work of contemporary builders by style and by the types of trees indigenous to each region—and it almost worked. To some degree, rustic furniture does reflect the distribution of tree species; manzanita and eucalyptus are usually found in California; "slash" pine is the result of logging in the Pacific Northwest. But there's a mountain maple in Colorado that looks like the eastern red maple and sugar maple; there are more than a hundred forms of willow in the country, and bent willow furniture appears everywhere willow does; a builder I know in the South works with white birch bark he gets from Minnesota or Vermont.

I kept running into this blurring, so I abandoned regional groupings in favor of style groupings, of which there are about eight. Magazines and books that feature rustic work are like the birds of the rustic world—scattering design seeds far and wide; consequently, an element of a chair design that may have first appeared in the Adirondacks now appears in a variation in California or British Columbia. In other words, all across the country, contemporary builders are working with a range of materials, in a variety of styles.

For this book, I received photographs of representative contemporary work that are clearly related to the furniture featured in my last book, *Making Rustic Furniture*. This collection is not so much a copy of that previous work as it is a testament to the nature of influence and the influence of nature. It speaks of trickle-down design, or of what Gustav Stickley experienced in the early part of the century, when his design innovation, popularly called "Mission" furniture, found itself reflected in the *Sears Catalog* and as the subject of many how-to articles in popular magazines, and even in his own magazine, *The Craftsman*.

There are personal, internal rhythms that send some people to the woods...as Noble Savage, neo-transcendentalist, Green survivalist, sculptor with Nature. In talking with builders I get a sense of strong personal mythology. We are acting out some compelling story line about how life should be lived, or might be lived, or can be lived. There are a lot of home-based, low-tech, we-cook, we-shop, we-raise-the-kids people who make the following collection of rustic furniture.

Historically, there have been many kinds of rustic wood furniture. Some use natural forms only structurally, as a kind of inexpensive framing material; others use natural-form materials in an ornamental way—either with a natural-form base or to decorate a base of milled materials. Almost all the styles fall into the following style categories.

*Stick chair, Daniel Mack*

# Gallery of Contemporary Rustic Furniture Makers

## STICK OR TWIG

*Stick* or *twig* furniture is made from branches and small trees, put together in a manner that imitates the proportions and lines of natural growth. Despite what the name and the appearance suggest, stick furniture is very sturdy. The wood is cut fresh and dried. There is very little or no reshaping of the sticks. Some builders use crooked sticks, while other prefer straight ones. Some leave the bark on; others peel it off. Stick furniture can be nailed together, fastened with dowels or with glued mortise-and-tenon joints. Usually there are few or no plans to follow; the maker remains flexible as he builds, working with the particulars of the sticks. The beauty and challenge is finding the right wood in the right proportions and making technically good joints.

*Above right: "Dear Scotland," Kay Kammerzell, WA*

*Above: pair of chairs at The Swag, Windle Dills, NC; inset, detail of chair*

■

50

I retired ten years ago from 25 years on the Phoenix, Arizona Fire Department. During my fire department days, I built and remodeled houses. I moved to Tyler, Texas eight years ago with my wife. I have been involved full time with wood crafts and rustic furniture making since moving here. I have a 2,500 square foot shop. I work alone and I do all the phases of the furniture making, from gathering the trees, peeling, bending, drying, design, and assembly. I have invented, designed, and built many of the tools I use. These include a tenon cutters, a bark stripper, a bending apparatus, and a rocking chair seat carver.

**William E. McCardle**

*Dining Room table and chairs and two chairs,
William McCardle, TX*

# Gallery of Contemporary Rustic Furniture Makers

I've always had a special love for woodworking. My woodworking, however, was more like carpentry than art until I discovered rustic furniture. I interviewed several Adirondack furniture makers and took hundreds of photographs of their work. The work of Barry Gregson and Daniel Mack is more sculptural than that of most rustic furniture makers; it has been an inspiration to me both technically and stylistically.

I use local eucalyptus and sycamore branches pruned from living trees. I like the idea that my woodworking is easy on our forests. Once I've decided to use a twig or branch, I study it for a while and get to know its particular proportions and shape.

The shape of each branch becomes a design element that I incorporate into the overall form of the chair. I use mortise and tenon joinery to assemble the parts. This joinery mimics the growth of a tree. The resulting chair gives the illusion of frailty when in fact it is quite sturdy.

So, in the final analysis, why do I make these chairs that mimic growing trees? Simply stated: I love trees. There is something about trees that calls to me. I used to climb trees as a kid and I enjoy sitting in them. My goal is to capture this feeling for trees in my chairs, so that when you sit in one of them, you get the feeling you're sitting in a tree.

**David Lee Sullenger**

*Three chairs, David Lee Sullenger, CA*

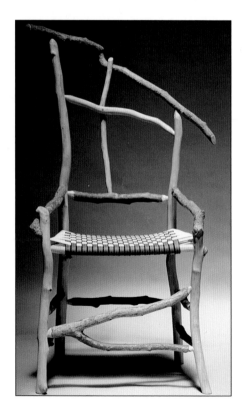

Top left: Manzanita armchair, David Findlay, CA
Below left: Picture frame, Nick Nickerson, NY
Below: Chair, Michael Armstrong, CO

# Gallery of Contemporary Rustic Furniture Maker

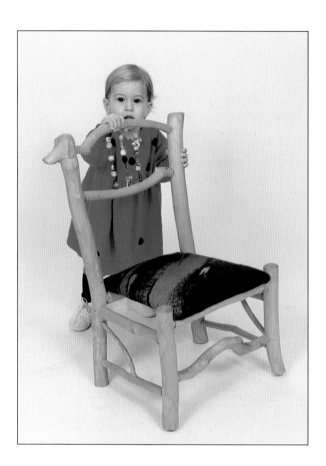

*Top left: Child's chair and Aja, ash, maple, beads, Tim Hayes, VT*

*Top right: Wall table, peeled and unpeeled corkscrew willow, Liz Hunt, OH*

*Below left: Crib, Jake Lemon, ID*

Blessed with a wonderful view of the Adirondack mountains, we start each day by considering the day's projects or the bounty that the woods around us have to offer. Our work seems heavily influenced by the changing of the seasons. In the spring, when the lilac is in full bloom, we find ourselves exploring old homesteads in search of twisted lilac. Old foundations, dead lilac bushes, and apple trees hint at what the countryside looked like 100 years ago. In the summer, our efforts are concentrated on keeping the gallery well stocked. Daily our minds are challenged by what to make of the roots, burls, and wild bends piled in our shop and pole barns. In the late fall, we start to harvest the wood stock that we want to keep with its bark on. In the winter, we spend our time down in our shop, filling the season's orders. Occasionally at dusk, we cross-country ski to the top of Beech mountain to enjoy the sunset.

**Barry Gregson, Adirondack Rustics**

*Crotch-back and burl chairs with cedar root-base table, high-back rocker with walnut back, and lilac settee, Barry Gregson, NY*

# Gallery of Contemporary Rustic Furniture Makers

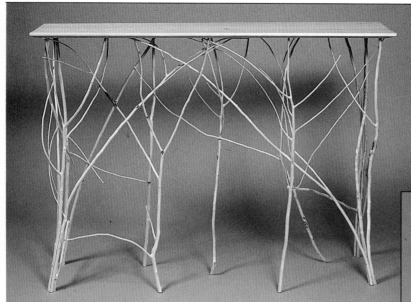

*Top left and middle right: "Floating" Table, cottonwood and pine, table with poplar top, Tor Faegre, IL*

*Below left: Forest Loveseat, willow, grapevine, and bird's nest, Liz Hunt, OH*

*Below right: Cactus Garden Bench, ribbonwood, David Findlay, CA*

Top left: Ironwood settee
with hickory bark seat,
Tom Lynch, WV

Top right: Red cedar dresser,
Hutch Traver, NC

Left: Settee and two tables,
Diane Cole, MT

# Gallery of Contemporary Rustic Furniture Makers

## TREES AND LOGS

*Tree* or *log* furniture is stick furniture on a grand scale. Logs are the materials for constructing beds and are often used for outdoor seating and for structures such as gazebos, pergolas, and arbors. Although the furniture may have a few smaller pieces for curves and bends, or a few roots and burls to add visual interest, it primarily uses large limbs or sections of trunks for structural elements. The furniture is substantial in look and weight.

For indoor furniture, any type of log will work. Lodgepole pine, aspen, and juniper are popular; white cedar is a good choice because it has low weight for its volume and is easy to work and finish. For outdoor work, black locust, white cedar, and redwood hold up well. The logs are usually peeled to minimize bug infestation. Handling techniques are more related to house building than furniture building.

In this log section, I have included photographs of furniture made from pieces of wood that fall somewhere between sticks and logs.

*Opposite top left: Settee, James Roth, VT*

*Opposite bottom left: Adirondack chair from roughwood, Larry Berger, CA*

*Opposite bottom right: Bed, William McCardle, TX*

*Top: Bed, Jake Lemon, ID*

*Above: Bed at The Swag, David Robinson, NJ*

*Right: 1950's style birch root chair, Larch Lodge, NH*

# Gallery of Contemporary Rustic Furniture Makers

Here's how we got started making timber furniture. Last summer, my partner Jeff and I moved into a log cabin deep in the northwest woodlands of Oregon. The immediate surroundings of the cabin were beautiful, except that one side of the property bordered a clear cut. The ground of this logging sight was strewn with tons of timber too narrow, crooked, or knotted to be profitably milled into dimensional lumber. The loggers typically gather and set fire to this beautiful wood, which they refer to as slash, producing clouds of carbon pollutants that fill the air. Gary, the cabin owner and a former furniture designer, knew that this wood still had a lot of life and beauty inside. It was during a walk through this vast clear cut, littered with slash, that the idea was conceived to use this slash to create an interior for the cabin. We began using slash in everything we made for the cabin, from furniture and doors to counter tops and wall moldings. Our experience creating each piece for the cabin was so enjoyable that Gary, Jeff, and I decided to become partners and create and sell slash furniture on a small-scale basis. We are excited about our current line of slash furniture. The materials in this line include slash collected from clear cuts, steel, tumbled marble, and slate.

**Jim Dobbie, Slash Furniture**

*Opposite top left: Bent log chair, Thomas Phillips, NY*

*Opposite top right: Lodgepole pine bed, Ted Ingham, Canada*

*Opposite left: Bed, Hutch Traver, NC*

*Opposite right: Shaker pine bench, Steve Weih, WY*

*Top right and middle: Slash bed with iron sunburst, slash sling chair, Jim Dobbie, OR*

*Below right: Bench, Jake Lemon, ID*

# Gallery of Contemporary Rustic Furniture Makers

### BENTWOOD

*Bentwood* is a very engaging style of rustic, created by bending and nailing long, straight, fresh branches or tree suckers around a sturdy, nailed frame. Unlike most stick furniture, bentwood is carefully planned and the builder uses dancelike motions to reshape thin wands into graceful curves, circles, and hearts. Supple, fast-growing woods such as willow, alder, and cottonwood are best suited to this style.

Bent willow furniture, commonly made in the southern United States, is one of the best-known styles. Making it is often a family affair, and designs are passed down for generations. The Amish in Pennsylvania, western New York, Ohio, and Indiana build another distinctive form of bentwood furniture that combines naturally formed wood and milled wood.

Following a course in willow basket-making in the winter of 1992, I was so enraptured by the wood's feel, smell, character, and bendable quality that I decided to venture further. In the fall of 1993, I asked my partner, Devone, for a how-to book for my birthday on making willow furniture, and he brought home Making Rustic Furniture, by Dan Mack. The creations and workmanship displayed by all the rustic makers were outstanding and inspiring.

We decided to try the plans for a chair by Michael Emmons, and began a cooperative effort of collecting and building. In a few weeks, after many adjustments, we had a chair! We could even sit on it, and had created it together, even though my tool-illiteracy just about did Devone in.

Since then, Devone has never looked back. The designs use his own triangulated frames for strength; the additional back support is intrinsic to each chair. He says that to be able to use natural growth and have it transform into something else is a feeling of "humble elation."

**Teri Signer**

*Opposite top left: Back view of bentwood chair, Barry Jones, GA*

*Opposite middle left: Twisted bentwood chairs and settee, Dan Quinn, NC*

*Opposite lower left: Willow and dogwood chairs, Tor Faegre, IL*

*Opposite lower right: Chair, Clifton Monteith, MI*

*Top right and middle: Willow and dogwood chairs, Devone Johnston, AB, Canada*

*Below left: Peeled poplar and willow settee, David Findlay, CA*

# Gallery of Contemporary Rustic Furniture Makers

## BARK APPLIQUÉ AND MOSAIC TWIG WORK

*Bark appliqué* refers to the style of gluing or nailing bark on top of existing casework. Popular barks include "white-paper" birch, golden birch, and fire cherry. The technique requires the care and patience of veneering.

Because there is a natural tendency of bark to curl, mosaic twig work is often nailed on top of the bark. There are beautiful examples of clocks, shelves, and sideboards in this style. The work is left unfinished or coated with a tung oil varnish.

The bark from birch and cherry can be harvested twice a year from live, standing trees. Done properly, the tree is not damaged and will continue to produce bark for years.

Mosaic work is also called *Swiss* or *split-work*. Small half- or full-round branch sections are combined in various patterns on top of existing casework, most often on tables, desks, or dressers. These pieces are usually nailed in place. This painstaking technique creates volume and intricacy, often with geometric patterns. Stunning results are achieved by using different woods or different forms of the same species.

My house is very close to the materials I need to gather. Birch bark, taken only from dead trees, is within miles. Red osier dogwood bushes, from which I prune several twigs at a time so that there will be more offshoots next season, are located along some of the country roads and railroad tracks nearby.

It's amazing how life unfolds before us. I would never have chosen this work out of college, but for now this is an ideal way to express my creativity, stay home for my child, and produce what I think is some of the most special furniture anyone could ever want in their home. I truly love what I do and am thrilled that rustic work has come into my life.

**Beth Humphreys**

*Opposite: Three clocks, Jerry and Jessica Farrell, NY*
*Opposite bottom left: Cabinet, Diane Cole, MT*
*Above and right: Picture frame, buffet, chest, Beth Humphreys, MI*

# Gallery of Contemporary Rustic Furniture Makers

*To God be the glory for our many talents and for providing us with the natural elements with which we can create and express our individual feelings.*

**Barney Bellinger, Sampson Bog**

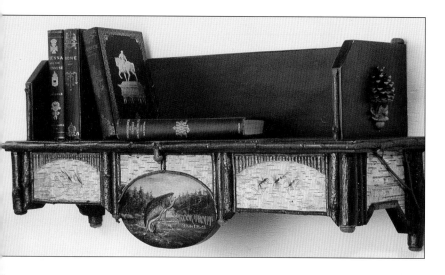

*Above and below left: Book shelf, table, cabinets, Barney Bellinger, NY*

*Opposite upper left: Birch bark used as a wall treatment, Daniel Mack, NY*

*Opposite upper right: Secretary, Dwayne Thompson, GA*

*Opposite lower right: Detail of antique frame, Ernest Stowe, NY*

*Opposite lower left: Birch bark frame, Nick Nickerson, NY*

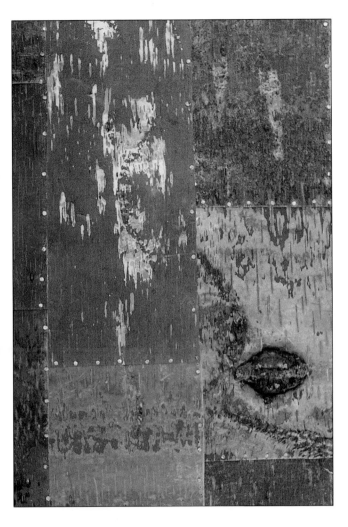

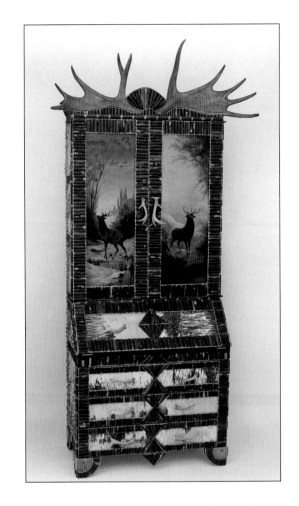

# Gallery of Contemporary Rustic Furniture Makers

### ROOT AND BURL WORK

This style uses the twisted, dense root systems of trees and shrubs to create chairs and table bases. The burls and galls growing on trees are used in similar ways. In the eastern United States, rhododendron or mountain laurel roots are used frequently; in the West, juniper is a favored wood. Often these materials are found as driftwood or as discarded wood on land being cleared for development. The wood must be washed thoroughly.

Strong technical and visual skills are required to combine these unwieldy, bulky elements into a well-proportioned piece of furniture. Some rustic makers split burls and polish the grain face for use as a table top. Others use the burled trunk or limb as a design component in stick or log furniture.

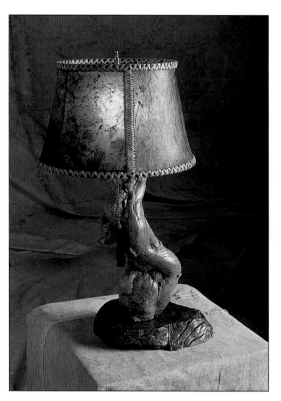

*Top right: Lamp, Jake Lemon, ID*

*Above and right: Root chairs,*
*Jerry Farrell, NY*

*Above left: Antique table,
private collection*

*Above right and below: two
settees, Larch Lodge, NH*

# Gallery of Contemporary Rustic Furniture Makers

*Above and below: Chairs, lamp, Brent McGregor (shown in workshop)*

## FOUND AND SALVAGED WOOD

*Found* and *salvaged* wood, such as driftwood, fence rails, and chestnut logs, has become more and more interesting to rustic makers. The wood has already experienced a history of use by the time the rustic gets hold of it (in one sense, rustic materials have always been "salvaged"—from the woodpile, the brush pile, and the compost heap). But there is a steady business in "reclaimed" wood such as barn boards and wood from various parts of old houses. Cheek cuts and irregular wood from sawmills have also been a rustic favorite. Lately there has been a growing interest in the use of wood reclaimed from the millions of pounds of discarded wooden shipping materials, chiefly "pallets" (see the discussion of furniture made from pallets in the materials section on page 84).

*Top right: Driftwood Adirondack chair, Jerry Farrell, NY*

*Below left and above: Driftwood headboard and beaver-chewed coffee-table base, Daniel Mack, NY*

# Gallery of Contemporary Rustic Furniture Makers

*Top left: Slab wood table, Daniel Mack, NY*

*Top right and above: Driftwood roll-top desk, table with drawer, Ted Box, MA*

*Middle left: Driftwood garden seat, Ian Jonson, NZ*

*Lower left: Fallen wood gate, Windle Dills, NC*

## MIXED MEDIA

*Mixed media* is a catchall category that includes anything left over. There is a strong tradition of furniture made from other natural elements: antler, horn, bone, and stone. But my focus in this book is furniture based on the tree form. There is a growing body of work that mixes the trees with other materials. That is what appears on these few pages: painted work and the use of some other natural and unusual found objects. Some makers are deliberately using recycled materials. I include this in rustic styles because the attitude towards the building is similar to that of the forest-bound rustic. Much of my work falls into this category at the present time.

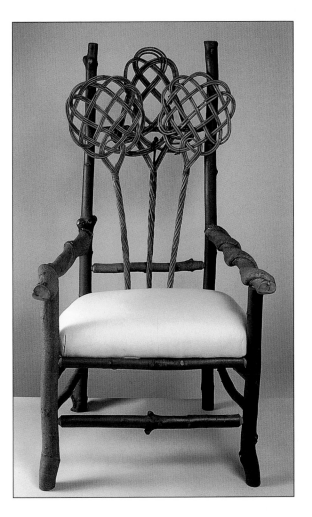

*Top right: Armoire, painted by Norma Smith, with fly rods, Dwayne Thompson, GA*

*Above right: Table, Jim Barnaby, MT*

*Above left: Rugbeater chair, Daniel Mack, NY*

# Gallery of Contemporary Rustic Furniture Makers

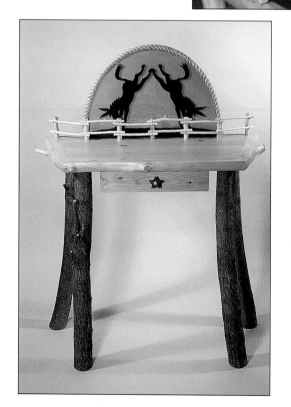

*Above left and detail: High-chair with glass beads, Tim Hayes, VT*

*Top right: "Ancestral Throne," Micheal Emmons, CA*

*Above: Bone Settee, Deb Gaffney, MT*

*Lower left: Table, Jim Barnaby, MT*

Daniel Mack used to make chairs like the one above. Now he collaborates on many pieces with other designers, such as sculptor and cabinetmaker Robert Kalka, who worked with Mack on the table and chairs shown below.

## EXPLORATIONS IN RUSTIC

Some makers come to rustic work looking for a style or object to make and remake. They are interested in the comfort and pleasure of repeating the same kinds of objects over and over. They work in a venerable tradition of craft people throughout history, all over the world.

However, there is another group of rustic workers who are not looking to ever make the same piece twice. They want the thrill of the hunt—not knowing if success or failure lies around the bend. In the six years I've spent collecting material between my first book and this one, I've come to recognize this second group of makers: I am one of them.

Here are a few more people whose work takes great leaps and lurches. Often the work has moved from daily utility to grand folly.

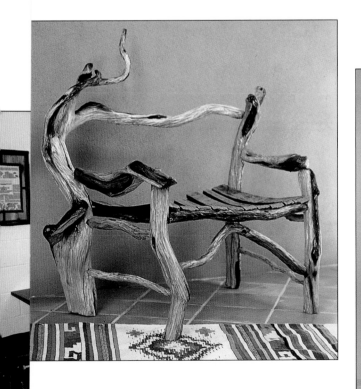

Micki Voisard, CA, used to carve chairs from manzanita (far left). Now she creates animal sculptures (left).

75

# Gallery of Contemporary Rustic Furniture Makers

*Judd Weisberg, NY, makes driftwood furniture (above right and left). But recently, he created a set for a dance performance (top).*

Michael Emmons, CA, built bentwood furniture
and replanted chairs in his early work (above). His
current work features stones and bones (lower left).

# Materials, Tools, and Techniques

The materials, tools, and techniques of rustic work have changed very little over the past 200 years. Basically, you just get some branches and saplings and fasten them together... Nonetheless, there are always new variations and details to discuss, and the ever-changing cast of characters who make rustic work continues to bring old and new information to our attention.

## FRESH WOOD

There are more materials available than ever. As farming practices have changed, more open land has been reclaimed by dense-growing trees. Only ten percent of the trees in a forest will reach maturity to become specimens; the other 90 percent are "thinnings" that retard each other's growth and have little commercial timber value. These are the trees often available for rustic work. Selective thinning, especially on the scale practiced in rustic work, hardly impacts the overall exchange of carbon dioxide and oxygen. The surrounding trees will branch and leaf out to fill the place and function of the thinned trees.

If you are lucky enough to live in a place where you are surrounded by woods, it's a good idea to scout them to see what types of woods are available. Often, different parts of a forest offer different varieties and sizes of wood. If these woods don't happen to belong to you, don't let that stop you: as long as you are not clear-cutting, I find that most landowners are willing to let you cut a few saplings on a regular basis. Of course, you want to avoid cutting wood that is an endangered species.

Most often, I cut the wood with a common pruning saw or bone saw; occasionally, I use a small chain saw. Because I have learned to "see" furniture in the trees, I cut only what I know I will use and rough-size it on the spot. I flush-cut the stumps to ground level and cut up and scatter what little I don't take with me. Like a responsible camper, I leave no trace of having been there.

Contrary to folk wisdom, I cut wood all year round. It's true that if you cut only in the winter, the sap in the trees is minimized, but I enjoy being in the woods in every season. When you are cutting skinny saplings and branches, you will not lose much bark, even if you cut wood in the summer.

*Above: Birch tree after bark has been removed*

## PEELED WOOD

*If you are interested in building rustic furniture with peeled wood, you definitely want to cut it at the right time of year—usually late spring to early summer. In the northeastern U.S., if you cut wood from mid-May through early July, the bark can easily be peeled off trees in long strips by using just a dull knife. If the wood is dry, or cut when the sap is down, peeling bark will be a long, arduous process involving a sharp penknife. You can use coarser tools such as a drawknife or a hatchet, but they nick and cut the wood, making it look more milled than peeled.*

*Above left: Daniel Mack peeled wood chair*
*Above: Daniel Mack peeling hickory bark*

# Materials, Tools, and Techniques

### RETRIEVED WOOD

The "waste" produced by many activities translates into a bounty of rustic materials. When "new housing starts are up," many acres of woodlands get cleared by developers; landscape services and tree surgeons are constantly pruning and thinning; farmers prune and renew their orchards yearly; local parks and highway crews are always cutting back along the shoulders of roads and often leave the trimmings there for a few weeks; commercial loggers take only the clear large trunk of the tree, leaving behind the top of the trunk and all the branches.

*A "slash" loyalist collects what loggers leave behind*

*Tor Faegre collecting buckthorn on the prairie*

### FALLEN WOOD

If you are the gambling type and are curious about insects, fungus, and mildew, you may want to take a chance on wood that has lingered on the forest floor or reclined in your friend's woodpile. Insects of all varieties make their homes in this type of wood. The results can be a bug infestation in your dining room or the disappointment of finding a spongy and wormy section inside a lovely log. Check the wood carefully; if you can't resist taking it home, be sure to separate it from your fresh wood and consider treating it before you bring it indoors.

The most damaging insects are the three kinds of wood-boring beetles—lyctids, anobids, and bostrichids. They find the starch in sapwood irresistible, and you will find them very difficult to chase away. The best solution is to leave behind any wood that has little telltale holes. If boring beetles manage to stow away in your newly collected wood, throw out any infested pieces as soon as you detect their presence. To persuade them to relocate, I've tried injecting turpentine down their holes; I've heated the wood with a heat gun or heat lamp until the beetles exit to find a cooler home. As a last (and rather unrustic) resort, you can fumigate the wood in a sealed chamber with professionally regulated fumigants such as methyl bromide and Vikane.

Driftwood is not likely to have bugs, but it may be a host for mildew and fungus. Heat or potent chemicals can usually stabilize this kind of wood.

## REGROWN WOOD

There are successful programs, chiefly in England, for coppicing wood for use in furniture. Coppicing is the procedure by which several new shoots or stems grow up from the stump or "stool" of a harvested tree. Willow is coppiced in the United States, and in Britain, sweet chestnut, ash, oak hazel, and willow have all been coppiced for centuries as part of the rural economy, providing fencing materials and other small-scale materials on a regular and renewable basis.

## REUSED WOOD

The reuse of wood is a primitive idea. For those of us raised in today's high-tech, throw-away world, reuse is both appealing and upsetting. The wood used for the shipping and packing of consumer goods has enormous reuse potential. The fact is that shipping wood makes up the second largest use of wood in the United States. Unfortunately, it also has a remarkably short life span; cut and assembled for a specific job, wooden crates and pallets become part, a large bulky part, of the landfill problem once that job has been completed.

*Above: Vince Appicella forming a pallet into rustic furniture*

*Left: A small "forest" of wooden pallets and shipping crates*

# Materials, Tools, and Techniques

The most common, ubiquitous form of shipping is the four-by-four-foot pallet, a sled on which small units are stacked, strapped, and shipped by truck. Beverage companies are one of the most obvious pallet users, but a vast amount of shipping wood is also used in the electrical and plumbing industries. Glass, steel, and auto manufacturers handle tons of odd-sized packing wood every day. Some of this get reused in shipping, but too much does not.

Pallets are made from either hardwoods—oak, walnut, cherry, maple—or from soft pine. They are almost always put together with pneumatically driven twisted nails, which accounts for their durability and resistance to easy dissembling. They cost less than $10.00 each.

Shipping wood is now one of the last frontiers for recycling and reclaiming, but there is very little secondary use for this wood and no incentive to reuse it. Much of it is so specialized that reusing or recycling it is more costly than buying new virgin-milled wood. As a result, there are piles of orphaned shipping pallets everywhere. What is needed is a shift in thinking about wood, as well as ongoing experimentation with reclaimed wood. We need to inform woodworkers and other builders and crafters about the institutional reuse of this wood. In landfills all across the country, this hardwood "trash" is just waiting for someone to transform it into beautiful, usable furniture and other objects.

The enterprising and visionary have turned this situation into business. Two New York companies, Haut House in Ithaca and the

South Bronx Redevelopment Corporation, also called Bronx 2000, have been developing designs that incorporate the wood reclaimed from shipping. I worked with Bronx 2000 a few years ago to demonstrate that reclaimed wood can have a second life as a building material. With funding from the Design Arts Program of the New York State Council on the Arts, I gave small stipends over a six-month period to ten woodworkers around the country to design and build functional objects—mostly chairs, tables, shelving, and small case-work—from reused wood. They proved that reused wood could be handled and reclaimed. The following photographs document their ingenious work.

In the few years since that project, there have been many art shows featuring recyled wood, and Bronx 2000 has taken one of the pilot technologies—a stacking or butcher-block technique—and is now in production with a line of what it calls "Environmental Classics": tables, lamps, and chairs made from reclaimed wood.

## SPREADING THE WORD

*If the idea of reusing shipping wood strikes a chord in you, here are some things you can do.*

▼ *Contact industrial arts teachers and offer to demonstrate safe techniques for how wood can be reclaimed and reused.*

▼ *Offer to provide designs for projects made from such wood—boxes, shelves, fencing, etc. In times of tight school budgets, the cost of virgin wood may be too high, and reclaimed wood may have a dollars and sense appeal.*

▼ *Start class discussions in the middle or high schools about reclaiming wood, and work with students to develop projects that use shipping wood donated by local industries.*

▼ *Share the stories of your successes and failures with other woodworkers in the pages of woodworking magazines. In these ways, we can begin to build a shared body of information that can serve to shift our attitudes towards the way wood gets used.*

Reclaiming of wood and the related product manufacturing can provide employment for nontraditional work forces in American inner cities and rural areas and in developing countries. There are plans to send containers of pallets to countries using wood as fuel to help preserve native forests and provide usable raw materials for handcrafts and low-tech manufacturing.

For woodworkers, the task is local—to keep reclaiming and reusing wood in our own work. Before companies such as Bronx 2000 emerged, some woodworkers had been doing exactly that—reusing the shipping wood they found in their town or city. They were operating in a time-honored tradition of frugal ingenuity: making do with what's available. Their woodworking ancestors at the turn of the century used cigar boxes and fruit boxes to make what's called and collected as "tramp art." Will this pallet furniture show up as collectible Pallet Art in the middle of the next century?

Often, in a piece of old rustic work, you will find a part of a fruit box or soap crate. Many rustic plant stands are made with tops from fruit crates. Much of Charles Sumner's work on pages 42 and 43 uses these materials.

*Opposite top right: Table and chair, Nicholas Mottern, NY*

*Opposite bottom right: Wagon, John Werner, CA; stand, Vince Appicella, NY*

*Top right: Table and chair, D.D. Drollette, MA*

*Left: Table, Daniel Mack, NY*

*Note: All these builders participated in the 1991 Skidworks Project in New York.*

# Materials, Tools, and Techniques

## STORING AND DRYING WOOD

Collecting the materials is just the start of the rustic process. One of the ongoing challenges is storing all that tree wood. If you plan to nail the joints, it is not as critical to dry the wood, so your need for storage is less acute. But if you plan to use the peg-in-hole method, technically called the mortise-and-tenon joint, you will need dry wood that does not shrink, warp, or twist. Here are a few comments regarding drying and storing wood.

Some rustic makers use small, commercially made kilns or solar kilns to dry their wood. Kiln drying extracts more moisture from wood than air drying. Kiln drying collapses the cells in wood, while air drying merely empties them of moisture. Kiln drying also arrests fungus and bakes bugs.

If you are air-drying your wood, keep in mind that wood air dries at a rate of one inch per year. That means that a chair post that is only 1-1/2 inches in diameter will take about 18 months to dry.

The key to successful rustic building is to have very dry rungs. If you use dry rungs, you can get away with using questionably dry posts. Holes (mortises) in the nearly dry posts will shrink around the more shaped ends (tenons) of the more dry rungs, producing a tight fit. This means that instead of having to plan ahead a year and a half with all the wood, I need to keep only a good supply of dry rung stock.

I use rungs that are less than 20 inches long. To accelerate the rate of drying, I rough-cut rung stock to this length and stack it on top of my barn or next to a radiator or on top of my furnace. Rungs are dry when they produce a clear, sharp snap when you rap them together.

Try to organize and label your stored wood to keep track of when it was cut. Rough-size the fresh-cut wood into useable lengths. Decide which pieces are rungs and which are posts. Then cut them a little longer than you need and tie them in bundles, or put them in boxes labeled with the date they were cut and their intended use. Although the spirit of rustic work is spontaneous and flexible, the secret to building on a regular basis is a well-organized collection of dry wood.

Here are some snapshots that show how different builders collect and store their rustic materials.

*Left: Twisted branches set out to dry*

*Opposite top: Steve Weih arranging lodgepole pines to dry*

*Opposite left: William McCardle's workshop*

*Opposite right: Daniels Mack's workshop*

# Materials, Tools, and Techniques

## TOOLS

A saw, a hammer, and some nails will get a rustic started, but much of the pleasure of this work comes from the ingenious application of tools and from finding special uses for tools in rustic service. Here are the basic tools you will need.

A pair of work gloves, safety glasses, a hand-saw (like the Stanley Short-cut), a tape measure, pruning clippers, a sharp knife, a drill (either electric or battery operated), set of bits from ⅛ to 1 inch (0.3-2.5 cm) (spade bits are okay for the sizes above ½ inch/1.3 cm), a rubber mallet, a rasp, a piece of chalk, a ball-point pen, a sturdy bench vise, a bottle of wood glue, and a box of Band-aids to prevent blisters.

With all this in an old five-gallon bucket, you could hire out as an itinerant rustic carpenter. When you want to settle down and have a "shop" you'll want to add the power tools you found in your father's basement:

A 10-inch (25.4 cm) chop saw, a floor drill press, a table saw, a work table or two (at different heights), and lots of storage room (lots and lots)

Seating for rustic chairs continues to be a challenge. I'm using more upholstery and woven Shaker tapes. Once in a while I use hickory bark that I have collected, or I purchase something from one of the seating suppliers, usually The Caning Shop in Berkeley, California. I suggest sending away for the catalogs and instruction books or videos from a few seating companies. Study the material and decide what kind of seating might look good on your rustic chairs and what kind of techniques you're interested in learning. The techniques of seating—caning, rushing, upholstery, and weaving with cloth or splint—are quite different from the building of rustic furniture; they take time to learn and accomplish, and each requires a different kind of fine motor coordination.

*Above: Barry Gregson's tools; note handmade wooden tenon cutters*

*Opposite top left: McCardle's hand made measurer*

*Opposite top right: McCardle's tenon cutter*

*Opposite right: Ted Ingham in his workshop*

## SAFETY

As with other types of woodworking, workshop and wood-handling safety are vital to the healthy continuation of rustic work. There are still traditional and preventable accidents that cripple rustics: the tree falling the wrong way on a rustic who didn't wear a hard hat...or fingers getting cut or cut off due to a momentary lapse of attention...or an eye with a bit of wood or metal in it because the builder forgot her safety glasses. Everybody knows about eye protection, fire extinguishers, smoke alarms, and first-aid kits in the shop...right?

There are other dangers specific to rustic work. Lyme disease, with its red bull's-eye rash is now a serious concern for rustics who thrive in the woods where deer ticks roam. And there are now stricter OSHA regulations relating to wood dust in the shop. These regulations usually don't affect the small shop, but the general concern for the long-term effects of wood dust is similar to the talk of tobacco smoke in the mid-1960s. For about $250, I recently added a triple-filter air cleaner to my shop. As we are all get-

ting older and smarter, such precautions will keep us in the shop longer and off a respirator.

Similarly, I use gloves when I'm applying any kind of finish to work. Boiled linseed oil contains dryers that irritate the skin; turpentine and paint thinners weren't made for regular contact with skin. Latex gloves give me protection and allow me the fine motor control I need. Most woodworking catalogs mentioned in the resource list on pages 137 and 138 now have fat sections on safety devices.

# Materials, Tools, and Techniques

*Above: Daniel Mack's workshop*

*Above right: Micki Voisard carving manzanita*

*Right: William McCardle bending back posts*

## GROWING PAINS

The day may come when you start getting more rustic work than you can handle. You'll want a bigger shop, a few helpers (employees or subcontractors), doubles or triples of all these tools, a dehumidification kiln (or two) to get stock stable quickly, an electric tenon cutter (with several heads), a reliable delivery service, an accountant, somebody to clean the shop bathroom, an answering machine and a fax (on its own line). What have I forgotten?

My point is simple: Get as many tools as you are comfortable with. Rustic work is not about tools. Tools are a distraction, (although an important distraction) from the real challenge of working beautifully with tree wood. The woodworking magazines, particularly *Woodshop News*, in Essex, Connecticut, can keep you informed about the range and source of available tools. In the resource section starting on page 137, I've listed information about tools.

*Top: William McCardle shaping a stick*

*Above: Chuck Fredricks finishing a child's chair*

# Materials, Tools, and Techniques

### FINISHES

*Changes in clean-air laws have contributed to new formulas of paints, varnishes, urethanes, and waxes. I, and many of my colleagues, still use tung oil varnish on both peeled and barked wood. On some raw wood, I now used thinned acrylic polyurethane, and I still like a 50/50 boiled linseed oil and turpentine mix on my barked forest chairs. Recently, my friend, painter and sculptor Sidney Simon, urged me to use a 50/50 mix of raw linseed and kerosene! I haven't tried it yet. He also recommended Renaissance Wax, which he says doesn't darken the wood.*

*Quite a few rustic makers have switched to the Livos line of finishes that are free of the lead dryers and other toxins found in traditional finishing materials. There is a hard oil finish, Meldos, which is good for kitchen applications and on furniture that children might gnaw on. I have used walnut oil as an alternative, but it doesn't dry as quickly. (See the resources list on page 138 for information about Livos.) The best thing to do is try, try, try.*

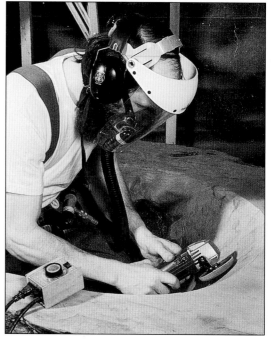

*Above: Brent McGregor sanding a log*
*Top right: Susan Bellinger applying a finish*
*Left: Barney Bellinger's workshop*

## MAKING MORTISE & TENON JOINTS

T he "peg in the hole" is the most "professional" form of joinery commonly used in rustic work. Here, using a very dry piece of wood, a tenon (or peg) is cut either round or square·and fitted exactly into a mortise (or hole) of the same size. But complications can arise when the mortise and tenon are not quite dry and stable. If a wet tenon shrinks as it dries in the hole, the result is a wiggle-waggle chair—not much good for sitting.

One way to get around this is to make sure the tenon wood is drier (much drier) than the wood of the mortise. Then as the inevitable shrinking proceeds, the wood of the wetter mortise will shrink more than the wood of the tenon, locking the hole down on the dryer peg. This is what's known as a "wet joint."

(This might be a good time to look back at the discussion of drying wood on page 86. You may want to force-dry some of the wood you'll be using for tenons.)

The most complicated technique to master in this type of joinery is cutting a proper tenon. It has to be a good solid fit in the mortise. So cutting good tenons is a challenge and a skill to be practiced. There are many ways to make tenons:

The *penknife* is a perpetual favorite. It's the obvious choice for your first attempts at tenon making and great for fine, careful shaping. It is also terrible for calluses and generally too slow for a production workshop. But penknives are portable, inexpensive, and simple to understand and operate. (They make for great "rustic" pictures—with you, the knife, and the stick.)

A *hatchet* can be used to fashion a rather crude tenon and is often preferable to a knife for log tenons and for preliminary shaping on larger sticks. The tenons are usually made quite long and often pass through and out the other side of the hole in the stock. Then the ends are often wedged or pegged through.

The *saw/chisel/rasp* is a one-two-three combination preferred by most people I teach in workshops. All three tools are inexpensive and readily available (and you probably have one of the three already). Using a saw, the rung is lightly scored around its circumference at the point where you want the tenon to begin. Then the tenon is chiseled away gently until it's almost the exact size. The final shaping is done with the rasp (or even a penknife would do).

The *hole saw* is an inventive, somewhat crude, power-driven method of tenon making. With the rung stock firmly clamped or set in a vise, a hole saw is attached to a drill press or a power drill and used to cut a tenon by drilling into the end of the stick. Then the remaining collar is cut away with a hand saw.

A few words of warning: Hole saws use big pilot drills to lead them into the stock. For cutting large tenons—over one inch diameter—this hole won't interfere with the structure of the tenon and can be plugged with a quarter-inch dowel. But for smaller tenons, there is a danger of removing too much from the inside of the tenon, thereby weakening it. Also remember that the diameter sizes for hole saws are gauged for the *outside* of the resulting hole. If you choose to try this method, be sure to measure the *inside* diameter of the saw.

The *plug cutter* or *tenon cutter* is similar in principle and set-up to the hole saw but is a finer cutting device that leaves no pilot hole in the tenon. Measurements are for inside cutting, and a saw is sometimes needed to cut away the outside collar. Tenon cutters are available from many of the mail order woodworking catalogs.

The *hollow auger* and *spoke pointer* is a hard combination to beat. This was the tenon-cutting method used by most turn-of-the-century carpenters. Both fit into a standard hand-operated brace. The spoke pointer—like a big pencil sharpener—tapers the wood to a point small enough to fit into the hollow auger, which is a two-edged cutter that makes perfect cylinders (tenons) of various diameters.

# Materials, Tools, and Techniques

Both devices are still available, but only from old tool dealers. When they're tuned up and working they make a great tenon and using them will give you good arm muscles. But be prepared to learn how to sharpen small blades and to spend some time tweaking this nice old pair of tools into proper working order.

A *rounder* is an early, hand-held form of the hollow auger. It's just a chunk of hardwood with a hole in it and a blade screwed on. You hold it in your hand and turn it around on the end of your pre-tapered stick. It makes a nice tenon. I've included a sampling of antique tool dealers in the resource section. Contact them for the hollow auger and the spoke pointer. The rounder is a less precise way to make tenons, but if you can find one...

A *lathe* can also be used for cutting tenons, but it's a big expensive tool with which I have had very little experience. When I have made tenons on a spring pole lathe, the results were quite acceptable. Some rustics tighten the chuck of a lathe onto their hollow auger and walk into it, rung in hand. (I've heard stories of hollow augers catapulting sticks through barn roofs.)

The *electric tenon cutter* is probably beyond the requirements (or budget) of the recreational rustic maker, but it is what I currently use to cut my tenons. For a substantial outlay of money I now have a motor-driven device with a cast-iron head that combines the actions of the spoke pointer and the hollow auger—just like the chair companies use. It's like a spoke-pointer with a hollow auger attached, or an electric rounder, a whirling set of knives. These specialized power tools are made to individual specifications in machine shops. I've listed the manufacturers in the resource section.

### MAKING MORTISES
Methods for making holes, or mortises, aren't as varied or inventive as those employed in tenon cutting. It's basically just a sharp drill bit in a hand brace or power drill. I've outlined these devices in the tools section.

*The most basic of tenon cutting tools*

*Tenon cutting with a hole saw*

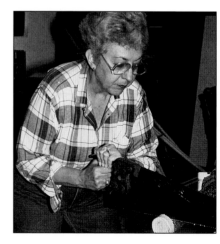
*Removing the collar left by a hole saw*

Left: Ian Jonson using a jack plane on a handled wedge
Above: Part of his workshop

## PROFILE: IAN JONSON, NEW ZEALAND

Ian Jonson lives in a Victorian-period house in Wellington, the capital city of New Zealand. He began doing rustic work in the late 1980s.

*I started using driftwood from the rivers and beaches, then I gave away all my power tools and resolved to use only hand tools, and to not buy any wood. Within a 50-mile radius of home there are several rivers. As the hinterland is covered in dense bush (too steep to burn and farm), there is plenty of driftwood, especially after a storm. The wood I like to work the most comes from the water, and is 100 percent saturated. My neighbors and friends supply me with branches and prunings to use. I work the wood wet and then let it dry before assembly, although with special items, I put them in a plastic bag and turn the bag inside out each 24 hours. This prevents the wood from cracking as it dries. I let the wood tell me what to make—the piece of wood will suggest an object by its shape, as I try to use the natural shape of the wood. I'm a "minimal interventionalist." I describe myself as a Rustic Woodwright.*

Middle: Driftwood drying
Bottom: Driftwood saddle stool, dried and beeswaxed

# Materials, Tools, and Techniques

**PROFILE: TOM LOESER**

Tom Loeser is a prominent furniture maker and designer who presently teaches at the University of Wisconsin at Madison. A few years ago, he took a course with me in Lake Placid. It was an unforgettable moment when the "unwoodworking" of rustic swept over Tom. He wrote me about the differences he saw between rustic and traditional woodworking.

*Woodworking, as I learned it, involved a certain amount of full-scale drawing, cutting lists, stock preparation, jig building, and other indirect techniques where the maker is not actually working on the wood that will make up the finished piece. The idea of working with the wood right from the beginning of the design process, and all the way through to the finished product, is very appealing.*

*The characteristic that I admire the most about rustic furniture is speed. When you know you will be able to finish a piece in a day or two, it does not become overly precious, and there is a willingness to try out new ideas. I have always been envious of the immediacy of stick construction. If you have an idea, you take the two pieces, and put them together. There is a freshness in work that is made as the idea is forming.*

*When I signed up to take the workshop, I thought I would learn some tricks and techniques about wood that I did not know. Instead, I found that there are not that many tricks, and it is more a question of having good aim with the electric drill. What makes a rustic piece good is not technique, but a sense of design and a willingness to figure out how to get the piece to fit together.*

*In some ways, I think rustic makers have it easy, because there are some givens, and they have a starting place. In a modern workshop, we start with square stock which can be like starting with a blank piece of paper. The builder has to have the ideas and impose those ideas on the raw material.*

*Working with sticks, the material can suggest things. When I needed a rail for the chair I was building, I walked over to the stick pile and found four or five sticks that would work as a rail, and each offered a different possibility. I also find rustic*

*Opposite: Tom Loeser building rustic chairs*
*Below left and right: Two of his rustic chairs and a detail*
*Bottom: Loeser folding chair, plywood, maple, stainless steel, and paint*

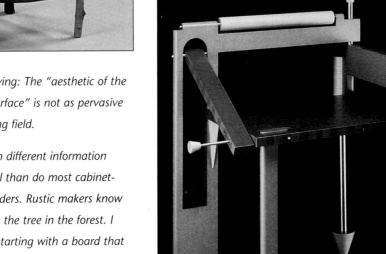

building to be quite forgiving: The "aesthetic of the tight joint and smooth surface" is not as pervasive as in the fine woodworking field.

I think rustic makers learn different information about wood as a material than do most cabinet-makers and furniture builders. Rustic makers know about wood starting with the tree in the forest. I know more about wood starting with a board that has been kiln dried and delivered to my shop from a lumberyard. Sometimes I am envious of that knowledge of the forest. I love the hickory furniture from Indiana, and one of my favorite details is the way they made bent pieces by setting them, when wet, over a fulcrum with a weight, and letting them dry into a strong, curved form. It's such an intelligent and direct use of the drying process in wood.

It seems some rustic makers, like some makers of cabinets and furniture, end up making the same couple of pieces over and over again. There is a cer-

tain appeal to seeing work by someone who has gotten very proficient at what he does, but I get more excited about pieces where the builder is exploring and trying new ideas. Those pieces have more personality.

# Materials, Tools, and Techniques

## PROFILE: DAVID ROBINSON

David Robinson first started building outdoor rustic structures when he worked with the Parks Department in New York City's Central Park. He now builds outdoor work for people all over the country, but chiefly in the New York metropolitan area. Here are photographs of one of his bridges at Winkler Botanical Garden in Alexandria, Virginia, showing stages of construction and the finished 24-foot structure.

## PROFILE: JIM DOBBIE AND SLASH FURNITURE

Jim Dobbie and his partners make light, clean furniture. But the photographs shown here offer a glimpse into the dark side of building with the "slash" that is discarded by commercial logging operations in Oregon.

*Top: Finished table*

*Above: Jim Dobbie cutting bedposts*

*Lower left: Early stage of a slash table*

# Materials, Tools, and Techniques

**PROFILE: NEWELS AND STAIRS**

In the Great Camps and other architectural marvels built about 100 years ago there is always a photograph of a tree forming the newel post on a stairway. Some use logs as the uprights, but others retain the grace and movement of the tree, even as they cooperate with the requirements of the local building codes. Here are a few examples that demonstrate the construction process and the finished work.

*This page and opposite page: Robert Kalka and Lou Tschopp collaborated with Daniel Mack on this applewood banister.*

I have had the chance to find and install a few of these newel post stairways. Here's one I installed in 1993 on an existing stair in a contemporary log home. The newel and bannister wood is apple and the balusters are maple forks; I peeled all the wood and let it dry for a few years before I began the work. The newel was leveled with a chain saw and portable planer and secured in place with lag screws coming up from the basement below. All the wood was finished with a Minwax oil finish.

*Right: Large applewood bannister, March Estates*

# Materials, Tools, and Techniques

## SELLING RUSTIC FURNITURE

Making tree furniture must not be confused with making a living from it. They are quite different and often at odds with one another. Anybody can learn to make a piece of rustic furniture...it's a wholesome and pleasurable experience. But to twist yourself up to design furniture to sell in the marketplace is like the difference between a sport and a commercial fisherman. Sure, the commercial fisherman might enjoy fishing, but it's only a small part of what his actual work is.

With rustic furniture, the "business" includes, but is not limited to:

work space with lots of extra storage space

a vehicle for transporting materials and finished work

an increasing number of tools, employees, or subcontractors

insurance and more insurance

rents, booth fees for shows, and travel expenses

advertisements and brochures

a fax machine

loans and bad debts

the services of an accountant

and maybe a lawyer.

You get the idea.

In addition, you need to have some angle on the rustic style that people want. You need a sense of design and beauty. Some of that comes from who you are and what you've lived through. But it also comes from reading, discussions, and visits to galleries, museums, and parks.

Finally, you have to understand the many different paths to selling rustic furniture: wholesaling to stores that find you at trade or craft shows; retailing at craft shows; running your own store; selling through galleries, interior designers, or architects. Much of my work is commissioned, which means people see a photograph of a piece I made and want something similar, but a little different. That starts a long discussion involving design, money, time, and how people see objects in their lives. I enjoy the heat of being in touch with the people who are going to own and use my work. Other makers want a store to handle

the selling for them. Each type of selling has its own set of rules and time frame. Each has its own cost and benefit as a way to do business. How you do it depends on who you are, where you live, and what kind of work you are trying to sell.

# Materials, Tools, and Techniques

## GOOD DESIGN IN RUSTIC FURNITURE

Even within the world of rustic furniture, the word "design" gets twisted around more than wisteria on a sapling. It seems people have pretty strong ideas about design—their designs, somebody else's, old designs, new ones...

The word itself has a variety of meanings. Sometimes "design" is used as praise; other times it conveys ridicule. Here are a few things included in the meaning of "design:"

the search for the perfect specifications

the most inventive use of new materials

the most ingenious application of traditional materials

the smart use of reclaimed materials

the wily use of third-world labor

the successful marriage of art and manufacturing.

I talk about good design when I get a can opener for a good price and it continues to open cans for years without giving me blisters. In other words, I am pleased by a number of its characteristics. Looking at the can opener doesn't give me pleasure; it stays in the background until I need to use it, but when I do—it doesn't let me down.

Good design in furniture is also a matter of different characteristics. It has to satisfy my internal sense of beauty. I have to be able to afford it and see a relationship between beauty and price. It needs to meet my expectations. A chair, for instance, has to look and function like a chair—keeping human bodies positioned 18 inches above the ground. It has to be comfortable for long periods of time or just short periods. Or perhaps it only has to imply a use for human backsides, but really serve to hold briefcases, keys, and cats. Its height or color may be more important than its relationship to bodies.

Unlike my need for a can opener, my "need" for a chair is complex. It operates on several levels at once. This chair is not background; it is foreground—very much a part of my public face to myself, my family, friends, and strangers. I will be judged by my chair. This is why there are hundreds of chairs on the market and not hundreds of can openers.

This helps explain the wide variety of "designs" in rustic furniture. People are buying different messages when they purchase different styles of rustic designs. Rustic tree furniture, like every other cultural artifact, is a code for something the maker or the buyer sees and wants to say about the world around him.

Design in furniture is all about the subtext of human life; "design" is a code word for a version of life right now. Look at the changing styles... The Milan show, the High Point show, the International Contemporary Furniture Fair. There is pressure to show something new... a new fashion, a bit of spice, sugar for the set design of daily life.

Good furniture design means being proud to display and use a piece of furniture. If you are a closet engineer who takes pleasure in the mechanics of the world, then sleek ergonomics is a key element in your sense of good design. If you are wealthy and proud of the number of different worlds you own or influence, then adventurous, expensive art furniture from unusual materials or colors may become part of the good design of one of your homes. If you are proud of having created a stable life for yourself and your family against a background of hardship and adversity, then new, sturdy, affordable department store furniture is "good design." If the pace of things seems a bit too fast, then a log home and bent willow furniture is good design.

The point is that each person is a set designer, introducing good design into their own lives.

That "good design" may come from Wal-Mart or Philipe Starke, but it functions in the same way: It is a statement to the world about who a person is and how he defines beauty and value. As lives change, as people age, as fortunes increase and dwindle, as families swell and break apart, the objects they collect around themselves become an ongoing and changing public statement of the human need for display of power, humor, comfort, conformity, or individuation. Good design is not just a list of specifications and materials: It reflects an understanding about the meaning of an object.

*Above: Chair, Daniel Mack, NY*

# Projects With Natural Forms

There are three personal dispositions that influence the way I do my work and discuss projects.

First of all, as with most rustics, I like working with what's around—the trees and scrap wood I find...the kind of nails, screws, and tacks I already have in my hardware drawers. For me, rustic work is essentially impromptu—not particularly planned. So, it is uncomfortable for me to tell you to go and get specific materials and supplies. I'd rather come over to your house and see what you already have.

A related second characteristic is that I don't like following plans. I enjoy the slight terror of not knowing how to do something "right" and yet to push on to get it done. So, why should I deprive you of inventing your own methods of work? Why should I pretend that my way of making something is the way to make something? I'd rather see the way you make it and then admire you.

*Top left: Bob Wallace making a chair*

*Above: Eliza Mack sawing a birch sapling*

*Opposite left: Judy Morrow drilling chair legs*

## PROJECTS FOR THE RUSTIC MINDED

*Suggesting rustic projects is sort of like teaching a sense of humor: You can talk about humor and you can tell jokes...but a sense of humor is more subtle and elusive...and a lot of it is finding your own style. There are several ways of thinking about rustic projects and many different reasons people want to try a project. Some want vocational training and believe that if someone showed them how to make something, they would be set. Other people aren't buckled as tightly to the "commodity" part of projects; they understand that "making" is a natural activity, one that helps them learn more about themselves and their world.*

*Rustic projects are great to do by yourself as a private activity. You may actually put a few sticks together, but as important, you'll be updating yourself on your own rhythms of work, frustration, ingenuity, play, and delight.*

*Rustic projects are also great to do with someone else. They invite collaboration, discussion, and amendment. And best of all, they are rich in memories: "...that summer, when you had that pile of apple trimmings and you built what one might call a chair. You kept making me sit in it!..."*

*Rustic projects make great presents because they are both from nature and from the hand. Nature is generous with its materials, and so we are encouraged to be generous with the fruits of our work. There is an ongoing generosity started by nature that ripples through to the makers and the users.*

Third, I first started making rustic furniture in a New York City apartment, so my sense of scale was influenced by the size of that apartment. Even 15 years later, I prefer to work with sticks that are no bigger than my fingers and wrists. They seem to have more life than logs, and I can move them around more easily. If I had worked as a logger or a mason, my sense of scale and space would be different.

These three biases inevitably lead me to suggest that some of you stop reading this section and go invent rustic work on your own. For those of you who persist in wanting to know how to duplicate a rustic item, be warned that the following projects are not ends in themselves: They are meant to provide the necessary encouragement to create your own successful rustic work.

# Projects With Natural Forms

### PROJECTS FROM THE PAST

In this first section, I'm presenting a series of projects from the past that I collected. Here are about a dozen ghost projects that your father, grandfather, or even great grandmother may have dawdled over on a Saturday afternoon. Notice how indistinct the "directions" have always been.

### 19TH CENTURY

For as long as there has been more than one person on earth, there has been someone to suggest a "project" to someone else. Popular magazines and books have been encouraging people to build rustic for more than a hundred years.

In the mid-19th century, there were many books, such as *The American Woman's Home*, by Catherine Beecher and Harriet Beecher Stowe, designed to instruct women on proper household conduct. Most of these had urgings and directions for building such rustic accessories as frames and baskets decorated with pinecones and acorns. But this essay from an 1878 book, *Beautiful Homes* or *Hints in House Furnishing*, encouraged women to become builders of rustic furniture, especially those women who may have lost their servants due to the Civil War.

*Cover of* Beautiful Homes *from which* "Veranda Chairs" *is excerpted*

## Veranda Chairs

The veranda or porch, be it ever so humble, should always be furnished with seats, for during the pleasant weather, these out-door haunts generally afford the most pleasant place for the family gatherings...

There are many varieties of chairs suitable for this purpose—iron, terra-cotta and handsome wooden kinds, but as these are all more or less expensive, we shall recommend the rustic seats as being not only appropriate but of easiest construction, and costing only the price of a pound or two of nails, and the labor of collecting or ordering a quantity of gnarled roots and branches of trees. In the country, a quantity of what are called "tree-tops," are easily obtained in places where wood-chopping has been going on, and nothing can be better for the purpose of these, covered, as they frequently are, with beautiful bark. Where it is desired to remove the bark, the pieces should first be soaked, when the bark

can be easily peeled off. Various patterns may be used for such chairs, several of which we give as a guide to some of our readers, and we would encourage any faint-hearted ladies by telling them that we see daily many perfect specimens of such chairs made by a lady noted for the beauty and delicacy of her hands. Furthermore, let us add, not only chairs and small articles have been thus made, but during last Winter she formed, in sections, an entire rustic

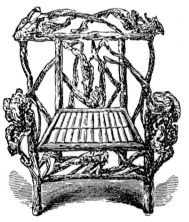

bridge, which was put together last Spring, and she is now engaged in constructing a lovely little Summer-house. This is done only at odd moments, for she has a large family and is one of those unfortunate persons who, losing the efficient help on which she had been accustomed to rely from her birth, during the late war, has found it doubly hard to learn late in life how to help herself, and perform her own household labor....We have digressed thus far, with the earnest desire to inspire our readers with an interest in this same rustic work...

We should say here, that rustic furniture is not suitable for furnishing any apartment in the house, not even the hall, inasmuch as it is a prolific source of dust and dirt, and a safe harbor for insects and "all manner of creeping things." If, however, any have a "warm love" for this style of furniture, let each piece be thoroughly cleaned and dried, then varnished with Copal....

Grape-vines, roots of hazel and laurel, branches of red cedar and spruce pine, with the gnarled tree-laps just mentioned, all afford fine material for this work, which will be found a fascinating employment, and prove far less arduous labor than would be imagined by most persons, who form their ideas of it from the pictures of the various articles which necessarily appear cumbrous and rough, but the more so the pieces are, the greater the ease of constructing.

# Projects With Natural Forms

Shortly after World War I, books started coming out urging men to go back to the woods, but to bring with them traces of civilization, as if to balance the barbarism and horror of war with a healthy engagement with nature. In his book, *Log Cabins and Cottages* (Forest and Stream Publishing Co., 1920), William Wick expresses this idea clearly: "We migrate to the woods, hunt and fish from choice; we go for change, recuperation, pleasure, health. We aim to treasure up energies in order to better sustain the tension of civilization."

The plans he presented were more dreamy than exact. Those reproduced here for a bed, a chair, a window seat, and a table don't have exact measurements, but they can provide inspiration to a contemporary maker; these are the kinds of images your grandfather pored over in the snowy winters of the 1920s. The chair on page 111 looks particularly low; I'm guessing the seat is drawn at about 12 inches. If you don't want to invent your own numbers for these projects, I've included general furniture dimensions in the resource section on pages 142 and 143.

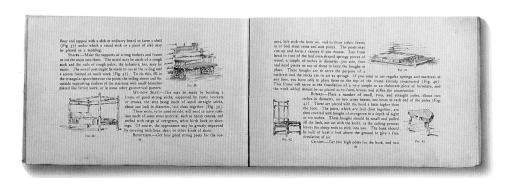

Log Cabins and Cottages, *from which the projects on pages 110 and 111 are excerpted*

### Bedsteads.

Get four good strong posts for the corners, left with the bark on; and to these either frame in or bolt stout cross and side pieces. The posts may run up and form a canopy if you choose. Lay from head to foot of the bed even-shaped springy pieces of wood, a couples of inches in diameter: put side, foot and head pieces on top of these to keep the boughs in place. These boughs are to serve the purpose of a mattress and the sticks are to act as springs. If you want to use regular springs and mattress at any time, you have only to place them on the top of the frame already constructed. This frame will serve as the foundation of a very simple or an elaborate piece of furniture, and the work added should be so placed as to form braces and stiffen the construction.

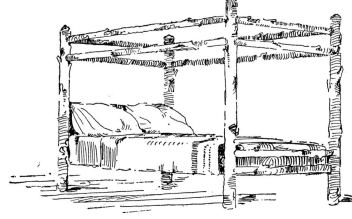

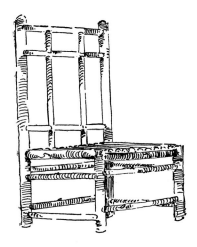

### Chairs.

Get two high posts for the back, and two legs of the height of a seat for the front. Frame in cross-pieces, as in the bedstead, and make the seat of small, straight sticks, laid close together, or stretch a stout piece of canvas or deer skin across. The usual bracing should then be made and the spaces filled with rustic work.

### Window Seat.

This may be made by building a frame of good strong sticks, supported by rustic brackets or crooks, the seat being made of small straight sticks, about one inch in diameter, laid close together.

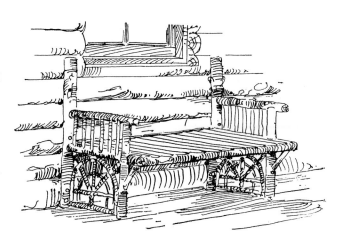

These seats, to be comfortable, will need to have cushions made of some stout material, such as heavy canvas, and stuffed with twigs of evergreen, white birch bark or shavings. Of course, the appearance may be greatly improved by covering with bear, deer or other kinds of skins.

### Tables.

To make a rough table, set four corner posts firmly in the ground, nailing cross-pieces on top, or make a framework like the bedstead. Cover the top with packing-box boards that you may have brought to the camp, or flooring, or pieces split out of soft wood logs; if of the latter, true them up into slabs. Nail cross-pieces on the table legs at the right height for seats, and let them extend out each side of the top; on these cross-pieces nail slabs or boards to form the seats.

The whirligig table is made in the ordinary way, with a rustic frame and a smaller table whirling in the centre on a pivot stick as shown in the sketch. On the whirling part you can place all the general dishes and each individual may be able to help himself.

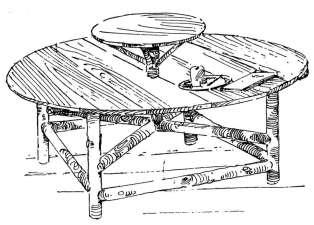

# Projects With Natural Forms

Every few months, during the 1930s, *Home Craft* magazine published plans for such rustic projects as "Rustic Willow Furniture," "Rustic Mail Box," "Rustic Garden Bench," and "Tree Stump Pedestal." Much of the drive behind the exhortation to the rustic came from a deep belief that contact with nature was the only counterbalance to the relentless, magnetic draw of the corruption and softness and muddle of cities and industry. Healthy fresh air and outdoor activities were the tonic for the blues of factory work.

W. Ben Hunt's book, *Rustic Construction* (Bruce Publishing Co., 1939) contains numerous attractive projects with clear and detailed instructions and illustrations, including the slab bench, table, and chairs reproduced here. Fifty years later, rustic makers are still making this time-honored furniture.

Rustic Construction, *from which "Slab Furniture" was excerpted*

## SLAB FURNITURE
### I. Materials

Slabs are the trimmings left after squaring up logs into lumber (Figure 1). In rural districts, there are portable sawmills to be found, where farmers have their logs sawed. Around these mills one can usually find a pile of slab wood from which choice pieces for making slab furniture may be selected.

If one lives in the city, there are always fuel companies that handle cordwood and slab wood, even in this day of oil burners.

The kind of wood varies, of course, with the locality. In the South, one may find slabs of cedar and cypress; in the West, redwood and fir; in the Northern states, oak, birch, pine, bass and the like.

If the furniture to be made is to be left out of doors, oak, cypress, pine, and cedar are the best. If it is to be used in a log cabin or on the porch, any light wood will do. The lighter the wood for indoors, the better, because then the furniture will be made of thicker slabs and will look much sturdier than if made of a thinner hardwood slab...Four feet is a good length for benches and tables.

*Figure 1*

Pick out slabs that run from 12 to 18 inches wide and from 3 to 6 inches in thickness at the thickest part. The bark, of course, is to be left on in order to add beauty to the finished piece. If benches with backs are to be made, pick out a few slabs about 6 inches wide and about 1 1/2 inches thick.

*Figure 2*

Saplings (Figure 2) for legs, arms, and stretchers, also are needed....If the saplings must be cut by the person using them, a trip into the country where woods and roadside brush abound is in order. Permission should, of course, be obtained from the owner before felling the saplings, and then the limbs and tops should be placed in heaps and not scattered all over the woods....

....Saplings should run from 1 to 3 inches in diameter, depending on where they are to be used....any solid saplings will do. Ironwood, elm, ash, or any wood of a tough character free from knots or at least straight, may be used. The branches and knots can be trimmed off if need be. The saplings may be peeled or left with the bark on. Since slab furniture is not made of measured lumber, the dimensions given in this article are only general....

## II. Tools

Most of these rustic pieces may be made with an ax and a bit and brace, but other tools, such as the hand cross-cut saw or bucksaw, a sharp hand ax, a drawknife, spokeshave, expansive bit, jack plane, a few chisels, a hammer, and a mallet will make the work very much easier. If one is handy with or owns an adz, so much the better. Slabs finished with a sharp adz and sanded have a wonderful appearance.

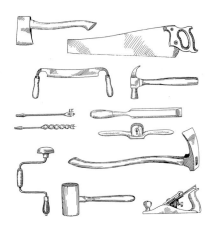

*Figure 3*

## III. Preparation of the Material

The preparation of slabs depends upon individual choice or ability. Some manufacturers of slab furniture run the cut side of the slab over a jointer and then sand it. That looks very

*Figure 4*

commercial and is not consistent with the bark that is left on the other side. Others run them over a jointer to level them and then plane them by hand to give them the proper touch. Another way—and this is the one usually used by the writer—is to plane off only enough of the rough sawed surface to get it smooth, leaving a trace of the saw marks. The large-toothed saws, especially circular saws, used for sawing lumber leave a rough surface with millions of splinters. After planing off the rougher portion, it is usually necessary to sandpaper the surface to remove these splinters. The edges and ends should be cut as shown in Figure 4. Edges and corners are rounded with a drawknife or spokeshave.

When slabs with rough bark are used, it is advisable to trim down the rougher part of the bark with a drawknife. White pine, hemlock, and tamarack bark, when shaved off, produce a surface of rich reddish brown interlaced with purple. The bark of yellow birch should be left as it is. The different woods found in different localities will need different treatment. However, when the bark is to be shaved down, lay the slab face down on a bench of some sort and clamp one end down, or nail a stop at the end nearest the worker. Then, with a drawknife, take off just enough of the rougher bark to give it a nice appearance.

*Figure 5*  *Figure 6*

Frequently, after slabs have been subjected to rain and snow, the bark loosens. This may be remedied by tacking the loose pieces down with shingle or lath nails after all work with the drawknife and bit is finished. Simply drive the nails wherever needed, then leave the slabs outdoors for a night or so, so that the nailheads will rust and in that way blend with the red or brown bark. If the bark is oiled before the nails are rusted, the heads will always appear unsightly.

The first thing to do in making the legs is to select one or more suitable saplings. Choose four pieces 17 inches long or longer and trim off all extending parts where limbs have been chopped off. This may be done with a knife or a spokeshave. Next, decide what size tenons are to be cut. As a rule, a little more than the bark of the piece having the smallest diameter is to be cut away. See Figure 5. Then set an expansive bit to bore a hole to fit this tenon. The other three legs are then marked with the bit as is shown in Figure 6. The holes in the slab must be bored with the same setting of the bit.

There are three ways in which legs or tenons may be fastened. Of course, if both the slab and the saplings used are well seasoned, one can simply put glue on the tenon and drive it home. But this is not the case in most instances. Therefore, it is well to use other means of fastening.

# Projects With Natural Forms

Figure 7

Figure 8

If a snug fit has been made, the leg may be driven home, and a large nail or spike driven in at an angle, as shown in Figure 7. This will do the trick, but there is no way of ever tightening such a leg should it loosen, except by driving another spike into it an another angle.

The blind-wedge method shown in Figure 8 is another way. The tenon should be fitted first, then a slot about 1 1/2 inches deep is sawed at right angles to the grain of the wood, and a wedge of hardwood cut to fit. The wedge is then set into the slot and the leg driven in place. The wedge spreads the end of the tenon and holds it firmly. When green saplings are used, another method may be employed by boring the hole from the top of the slab all the way through, as is shown in Figure 9. If this method is used, the tenon is cut so that about 1/2 inch protrudes through the hole. Remove the leg and saw a slot down the center of the tenon and again drive it in place. Then drive a wedge in from the top and saw it off flush with the seat. Then when the wood dries and the legs loosed, the wedge may be driven in farther or a thicker wedge put in place of it. Where slabs are quite thick, holes may be bored and dowels driven in, as shown in Figure 10.

Figure 9

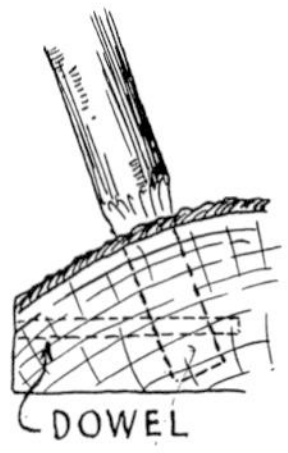

Figure 10

Figure 11

To fasten the rungs, use nails as was done for fastening the legs, or bore holes through them and tie them in place with rawhide thongs, as shown in Figure 11. The thongs should be cut 1/4 to 3/8 inch wide and soaked for about 12 hours before using. Pull them up as tightly as possible and conceal the ends. When the rawhide dries, it will shrink and hold for ages, provided no dampness reaches it. Varnishing it will help to keep dampness out. This method gives the furniture an added pioneer touch.

## IV. Finishing Slab Furniture

To finish furniture of this type, the first requirement is to bug proof the bark. A thorough brushing of 3 parts boiled linseed oil and 1 part turpentine will take care of this. If the furniture is to be left outdoors, do not use this oil on the worked surface of the slab, as it tends to turn dark in time. Outdoor furniture stands up better if the slab tops are given several coats of spar varnish. For indoor use a light coat of walnut stain, thinned down with turpentine and a coat or two of shellac or varnish will do very nicely on the raw wood. The bark on indoor furniture, too, should be given a good brushing of linseed oil and turpentine.

Sometimes the legs, rungs, and stretchers are made of peeled saplings. If the bark does not peel readily, it may be cut away with a drawknife. These peeled rounds should be finished the same as the slab tops.

## V. Making a Bench

Select the slab that is to be used for the seat. Since the legs of these benches are usually set at an angle, it is well to make a jig, such as is shown in Figure 12, to act as a guide in boring the holes. The distance that the leg is set in from the edge and end of the slab depends upon the conditions. With thin slabs, it is best to bore

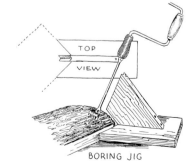

Figure 12

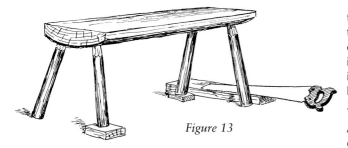

Figure 13

the holes farther from the edge than on thicker slabs. For the average slab, the center of the hole should be about 4 1/2 inches from the end and from 2 1/2 to 3 inches from the edge. The angle on the boring jig should be between 15 and 20 degrees.

Assemble the bench as has already been described. After the legs have all been fastened into the slab, the bench will require leveling. Set it on a level table or on the floor and level it up with small pieces of wood placed under the shorter legs as shown in Figure 13. Then use a piece of lumber of the right thickness as a saw guide (see Figure 13). Saw halfway through each leg, then turn the bench on its side and finish sawing off each leg.

If rungs and stretchers are used, they should be thinner than the legs and the holes, and tenons should be 1 inch or even smaller if small saplings are used. When making a bench with rungs and stretchers, bore the holes, fit the legs and level off as before mentioned.

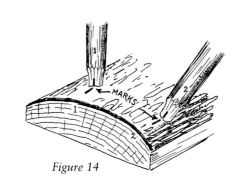

Figure 14

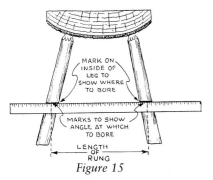

Figure 15

Mark each leg as shown in Figure 14 with yellow crayon, so that it can be put back in the same position. Measure up 6 to 7 inches from the end of each leg and mark. Then place a rule as shown in Figure 15 and draw a line along it. This gives the proper angle for the boring. Then mark the place on the inner side of each leg to show where to bore. Lastly, measure how long the rung is to be, measuring from the center of each leg, as shown in Figure 15. When ready to assemble, fit the legs and rung together first. Then drive the legs into the seat or slab, and fasten everything. Rungs, as a rule, need no special fastening, but a 3/8-inch dowel or a nail will always help to keep them in place, especially when the bench is to be left outdoors.

If a stretcher is to be added (see Figure 16), fit the legs and rungs on each end temporarily and then measure the length of the stretchers. As the rungs may be turned without changing anything, bore the holes for the stretcher ends in the center of each rung without any special marking.

Fasten two lengths with their rung in place at one end of the bench. Then assemble the other two legs with the rung and stretchers. Set them in place and drive everything together solidly. Dowels or nails may be used to fasten the ends of the stretchers.

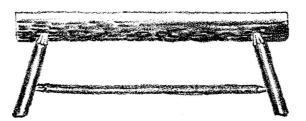

Figure 16

# Projects With Natural Forms

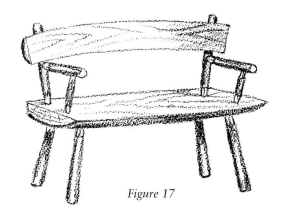

*Figure 17*

## VI. Backs

Figure 17 shows a bench with back and armrests. The armrests may be left off, but they add considerable strength to the back. Figure 18 shows front and end views of such a bench. Note that the arms are set out farther to the edge of the seat, and should be set at a slight angle outward and foreward. Smaller slabs are used for the back, and if one can be found with a curve to it, so much the better. The side view shows how the back is set into the upright.

The uprights are fastened into the slab just as is done with the legs. Then the back is simply set in and nailed on. Two narrow slabs may be used for the back instead of one wider one.

Figures 19 and 20 show another method of fastening back and armrests to the bench.

## VII. Tables

Rustic tables are usually made for outdoor use and therefore should be made of wood that will withstand the weather. For indoor tables, use the lightest wood to be found such as bass, pine, or some other light local wood. Tables are usually 30 inches high, while top sizes depend upon what they are to be used for, and the material that is procurable or on hand.

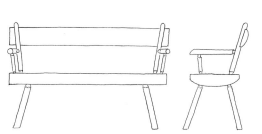

*Figure 18*

*Figure 19*

Table tops should be planed down quite smooth. They are usually finished with two or more coats of spar varnish. Figure 21 shows a table made from a single wide slab. (In the author's locality, a wide slab is about 20 inches wide and about 5 inches in the thickest part.) The table is made as though it were a bench, 30 inches high. The legs for such a table should be about 3 inches in diameter at the thickest end.

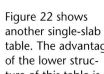

Figure 22 shows another single-slab table. The advantage of the lower structure of this table is that the legs will not sink into soft ground. The uprights are mortised into the top and set into the lower crosspieces. The crosspieces are logs split or sawed in half. The braces shown in the illustration may be fastened with nails or spikes as shown.

When a wider table is wanted, use two or three slabs for the top. To make a table of the type shown in Figure 23, plane the slabs to a smooth surface, and cut the edges square and straight. A piece of 4-inch sapling ripped down the middle will make satis-

*Figure 21*

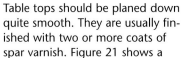

*Figure 20*

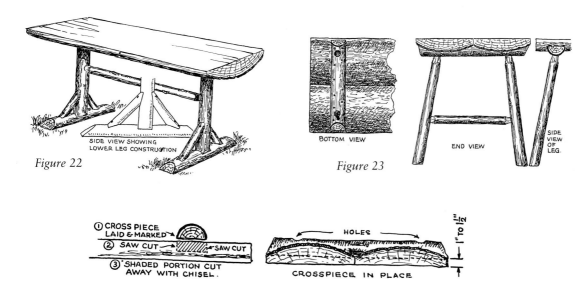

Figure 22

Figure 23

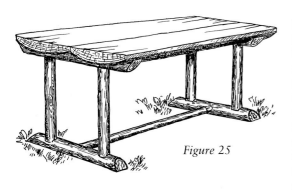

① CROSS PIECE
LAID & MARKED
② SAW CUT ← → SAW CUT
③ SHADED PORTION CUT
AWAY WITH CHISEL.

HOLES

CROSSPIECE IN PLACE

1" to 1½"

Figure 24

Figure 25

factory crosspieces. To fit the crosspieces, place the slabs, smooth side down, side by side, with the crosspieces in place. Mark the location of the crosspieces with yellow crayon. Saw along these marks to the depth shown in Figure 24, then cut out the dado with a wide chisel. Measure the remaining wood at each edge to make sure that the top pieces will be even. Before nailing the crosspiece in place, determine where the legs are to be placed and mark. Then proceed to nail, spike, or screw the crosspiece in place. If the top should not be even, a little planing will soon remedy the trouble. The table top is then ready to be placed on any sort of base. Figure 23 shows a simple method. The legs are made of 3-inch saplings.

## VIII. Chairs

Chairs require slabs that are wider than those used for benches. It is well, therefore, to save the wide slabs especially for the purpose of making them. Chairs for indoor use may be made of softwood. Those to be exposed to the weather had better be made of hardwood.

Figure 26 shows a chair made by the same methods employed for making benches, except that the grain in the seat is made to run from front to rear, and that the back is made higher than those put in benches. The depth of the seat should be from 14 to 16 inches, and the angle between the seat and the back from 100 to 110 degrees.

Figure 27 shows another type of chair, the seat and back of which are both made from the same 4-foot slab. Cut the slab in two as shown in Figure 28. Next cut the tenon on the longer piece, which is to be used for the back. This tenon should be 3

Figure 26

Figure 27

# Projects With Natural Forms

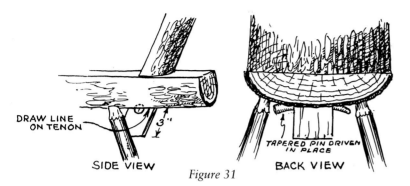

DRAW LINE
ON TENON

3"

SIDE VIEW

*Figure 31*

TAPERED PIN DRIVEN
IN PLACE

BACK VIEW

inches longer than the thickness of the seat slab and 3 inches wide. Slabs wide enough for chair seats are usually 3 to 4 inches thick, hence the tenon will roughly be about 3 inches square. Cut the shoulder at an angle of 70 to 80 degrees, as shown in Figure 29.

Measure back 14 inches from the front of the seat. See Figure 30, and cut a mortise to fit the tenon. Be careful to cut it at the same angle as that used for the back. Then assemble the back and seat, and draw a line on the tenon to denote the thickness of the seat. See Figure 31. Take the two pieces apart again and bore a 1-inch hole through the tenon, using the line just drawn as the center, as shown in Figure 31. Next make a hardwood draw pin about 5 inches long, tapering from 1 inch to 7⁄16 inch.

The legs should be set in place before fastening the back to the seat, as it is easier to bore the holes if the latter can be laid flat on the floor. Figure 27 shows the position for the legs.

The back is then set in place and the draw pin driven through the hole. Start the pin carefully and drive it in place as shown in the back view of Figure 31. This draws the back down firmly, where it will be held indefinitely in this position. When leveling up the legs, set the chair at a comfortable angle and then mark and cut them. The seat should slope slightly from front to rear, and the back legs should be given slightly more slant than the front ones.

A simpler method of making a slab chair is to fasten the back down to the seat with 3⁄8 inch lag screws as shown in Figure 32. Determine where the back is to be placed on the seat and bore two 3⁄8 inch holes through the seat.

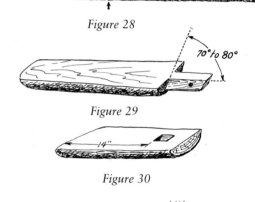

20"        28"

*Figure 28*

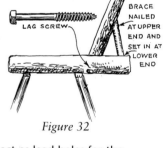

70° to 80°

*Figure 29*

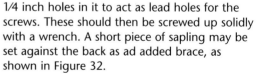

14"

*Figure 30*

LAG SCREW

BRACE
NAILED
AT UPPER
END AND
SET IN AT
LOWER
END

*Figure 32*

Then with the back held in place, bore 1⁄4 inch holes in it to act as lead holes for the screws. These should then be screwed up solidly with a wrench. A short piece of sapling may be set against the back as ad added brace, as shown in Figure 32.

Chairs of this type may be made quite comfortable by shaping the seat and the back as shown in Figure 33. This requires extra work with an adz or chisels but it is well worth the effort. This shaping must, of course, be done before the final assembling.

*Figure 33*

## COLD WAR RUSTICS

Just because a project is old, doesn't mean it can't be stupid. When I found the following cards, my memory flooded with school mornings in the early 1950s. My Shredded Wheat was packaged in layers, separated by cardboard cards that purported to teach "Injun-uity" to us budding cold warriors. They offered plans for obscure projects that required lashing, sewing, and carefully splitting 15-foot-long and 5-inch-wide maple saplings! As an eight-year-old, I didn't have ready access to yards and yards of canvas, so

I went off to my suburban school feeling like an anglo idiot, angry with my parents for not needing sheep fences, sleds, or portable couches. One quick glance at these projects will tell you why I waited another quarter century to make my first rustic project .

## PROJECTS (ALMOST) WITHOUT TOOLS

*"I hate sharp noisy tools...What can I make?"*

Making is pretty much about the use of tools, but there is an important part that has to do with seeing, finding, selecting, and relocating. A good example is what people "make" on a trip to the beach; they often make a collection of rocks or driftwood or beach glass. They see and select elements from a natural environment and put it in another setting. If you walk in the woods often enough, you're bound to come home with a walking stick; by recognizing that the shape and size of a fallen branch will "make" a good walking stick, you're exercising the same ability as a rustic who can "see" the finished chair in the tree.

Another way to exercise this "seeing" is to photograph or draw trees, a bird, or a pinecone in a natural setting. This activity includes some tools— paper/pencils, camera/film—but not the sharp, noisy ones. This is a good way to practice selecting and combining elements, a key feature of rustic work.

You can also select and recreate a tiny bit of the natural environment by making a terrarium or a moss and fern arrangement, or by transplanting a small tree from the woods to your backyard. There are many books on the Japanese art of *ikebana*, which relates to the visual skills of rustic work more than to the construction skills.

# Projects With Natural Forms

## RUSTICATING: PICTURE FRAMES AND MORE

Rusticating is the process by which an already constructed piece—a chair, dresser, table, picture frame, or mantel—is decorated, remodeled, or restyled in a rustic manner, using one or several rustic techniques.

Rusticating a frame is a great starter project. You skip the construction and move ahead to the finer detail parts. In the process, you quickly experience what is key to rustic style: You get to make an object that has visual and tactile appeal; its surface looks and feels inviting.

It is often not necessary to have the hidden construction of a rustic piece actually be made from nonmilled materials. So, rusticating also gives the maker a chance to question just how much of a project has to start with trees. For instance, almost all birch-bark applique work is done on top of "regular" casework made by skilled carpenters and cabinet makers. The various barks and trim are then applied on the surface. The gallery section on pages 64-67 has a number of examples of this.

The little project shown on page 120, easily accomplished in less than a hour, simulates that process. Slip a favorite picture in a plain wooden frame. In this case, I used a framed reproduction of a Currier and Ives summer scene. With a few strips of birch bark, a few twigs, a handful of pinecones and lichen, and a sprig of pine, the static oak frame is enlivened. Use regular wood glue as the adhesive.

You can also rusticate a premade wooden frame by nailing or gluing on small sticks.

Here's a more ambitious and lengthy bark project that I work on when I have a few extra hours. I purchased a Mission-style arm chair; it's not a Stickley, not very valuable, but it's mine and it's comfortable. I've been peeling very thin—almost tissue-thin—layers of birch bark and gluing them onto the faces of all the wood. First I rough up the surface of the wood and then use wood glue to hold the bark on. Then I clamp the bark to the chair until it dries, slipping a piece of waxed paper in between the clamp and the surface. What I like about this design is the unexpected combination of the squared forms of the chair and the treelike surface.

## RUSTICATING A PLANTER

I went to the local garden store and bought a deck planter for under $20.00. It was well-made; it would have taken me longer in time and materials to make my own.

I collected a pile of fresh cuttings from the yard...tree trimmings and a few pliable shrub stakes. The tools were very simple: a saw, clippers, a hammer, and a few nails.

First I decided to put legs on the planter; I chose short legs. (Long legs would have made it a standing porch planter.) After attaching the legs, I began to decorate the sides with both plain and fancy parts of branches. Finally, I decided to edge the whole planter with half-round cuts, made by clipping short sections of branches in half length-wise. The first one of these I made has lasted six years so far, sitting out on the ground all year long.

This project offers you the chance to explore various rustic materials and techniques. You can cover a planter with bark or roots, mortise in the legs, nail on graceful bentwood wands, or screw chunky half-logs onto the side. It's your choice.

# Projects With Natural Forms

### CURTAIN RODS / TOWEL RACK

This is a very good project because it's a blend of found wood and simple construction—all in the service of something very useful.

This is a good make-it-in-the-woods project or one that is easy to do when there are lots of trees being thinned or pruned. The major challenge is visual. You have to spy the right combination of a diameter and an angle. As I've said before, this visual skill is the basis of all good rustic work.

My eight-year-old, Eliza, and I were at a workshop where there was a pile of birch saplings. She wanted to "make something," so we got a saw and the clippers and half an hour later she had the pieces of a curtain rod arrangement just like the one her sister has.

We took the sections to the workbench and she flattened off the back of the supports with a rasp. She also used the rasp to remove any sharp knobs or branch scars.

Screws hold the supports on the wall and keep the rod in place. One of these supports can be used as a coat hook and the same design can be adapted for a towel rack.

### MORTISE AND TENON RUSTIC TOWEL RACK

Here's another towel rack design that involves mortise and tenon joinery.

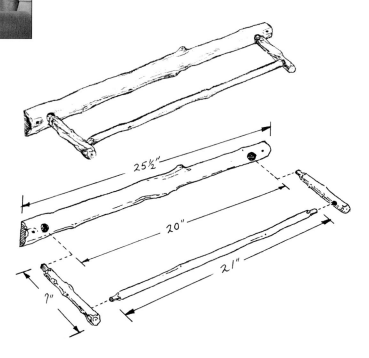

25½"

20"

21"

?"

## TREE SETTEE

I found this old photograph of a young man sitting in a chair built in and around a small tree. It looks like you'll have to put 11 nails into the tree to make this work. My forester friends say this should not harm the tree. I've adapted the chair as a two-seater, with room for a person on each side of the tree trunk.

### Materials

Dry or green saplings:

5 rails for seat and back, 54" (135 cm) long,
   1" x 3" (2.5 x 7.5 cm) diameter

2 seat/back diagonal supports, 60" (150 cm) long,
   1" x 3" (2.5 x 7.5 cm) diameter

4 arms/top diagonal, 40"(100 cm) long,
   1" x 2" (2.5 x 5 cm) diameter

### Tools and Supplies

saw

hammer

electric drill and bits

rasp

24 4" to 5" (10-12.5 cm) nails

36" (90 cm) heavy-gauge wire

### Procedure

1. Predrill three holes in the center of each rail. Make each hole just bigger than the nails you are using.

2. Nail three of the rails into the tree as indicated (Figure 1).

3. Nail and lash the diagonal back supports in place with the heavy-gauge wire.

4. Nail the two final seat rails onto the diagonals (Figure 2).

5. Add arms to the front seat rail and to the top rail on the tree.

6. Add diagonals to steady up the top rail and the arms to tree.

7. Smooth off any sharp edges with the rasp.

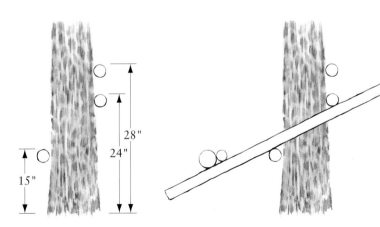

Figure 1          Figure 2

# Projects With Natural Forms

## RUSTIC SIDE TABLE
### (2 to 4 hours)

These next three projects require more from the maker in terms of time and tools, but they are both easy to do.

### Materials

1 piece of wood for the top, at least 10" x 10" (25 x 25 cm) and 1" (2.5 cm) thick

4 legs, 20" (50 cm) long by about 1-½" (3.8 cm) in diameter

6 branches for cross braces, about 12" (30 cm) long and 1" (2.5 cm) wide

### Tools and Supplies

hammer

drill, ¾" (1.9 cm) bit and bit for nail holes

1-½" (3.8 cm) nails

whittling knife

handsaw

materials for decoration: paint, tacks, old trim, wallpaper, wrapping paper, etc.

### Procedure

1. About 2" (5 cm) in from each corner of the top, drill a ¾" (1.9 cm) diameter hole at least ¾" (1.9 cm) into the wood. Tip the hole

slightly to the outside so that the legs splay. If you have to drill through the top, that's o.k.

2. Whittle the ends of the legs to ¾" (1.9 cm) pegs so that they fit in the holes. Put all the legs in the holes and turn and adjust them until they look right.

3. Once you're satisfied with the look of the legs in the top, begin to nail cross pieces between all the legs. Predrill holes for the nails. These can go around in a box style, or diagonally across the inside, or both. Use as many or as few as looks good to you.

4. After the basic table frame is made, level the legs by placing the three even ones on the table and let the long one hang off the edge. Cut that edge off. Another approach is to put the whole table in a pan of water and cut each leg off at the watermark. Now it is time to decorate.

5. Options: Limited only by your time and taste. The top: paint, wallpaper, fabric, bark—glued or tacked on with copper or upholstery tacks, dominoes, bottle caps, or poker chips.

The sides: pieces of twig, bent split, rounded or pointed, each painted a different color.

# Projects With Natural Forms

### MINIATURE CHAIR

**Materials**

3 lengths of straight, dry wood, 4'
(1.2 m) long, tapering from ¾" to ⁵⁄₁₆"
(1.9-0.2 cm) in diameter

**Tools and Supplies**

handsaw or clippers

pencil

vise

drill and small drill bit

whittling knife

string

wood glue

**Procedure**

1. The back panel is constructed from two back posts, each 12" (30 cm) long, and four rungs, each 3-½" (8.9 cm) long (smaller diameter than the posts). Look through the available wood and choose a few pieces of wood that seem to go together in size, texture, or shape. Cut the two longest to 12" (30 cm) and position them in a way that pleases you.

2. Mark arrows on the bottom of the posts to indicate the axis along which you want to put your rungs. Along these axes, put marks

up from the bottom at 1-½", 3-½", 4-½", and 9-½"(3.8 cm, 8.9 cm, 11.4 cm, and 22.5 cm).

3. With the post held firmly in a vise, drill holes at the marked points. Make the holes no bigger than half the size of the post itself, e.g., a ¾" (1.9 cm) post gets holes ⅜" (1.0 cm) in diameter. Drill the holes about halfway through the post. (OOPS... we can repair any holes that go all the way through. Mistakes are opportunities for innovation.)

4. Whittle only two rungs to fit into the two center holes of the back posts. No, they cannot be loose, nor pointy; we need a nice, tight squeaky fit. Keep trying until you have whittled a pair of good-fitting rungs. Fit these into the back posts. Are the missing two rungs (the top and bottom) going to be the same length as the center two? Probably not...maybe a little bigger or smaller. So figure out the length you need for the remaining two and whittle all the ends to fit the holes.

5. Assemble the back and look at it. Do you need to make any changes? If so, make them. If not, carefully pull the back apart and glue each rung into the back posts. Tighten up the back with a tourniquet of string. Let it dry while you make the front panel.

6. The front panel is made from two posts, each 5" (12.5 cm) long, and two rungs, each 4-½" (11.4 cm) long. Repeat steps 1 through 5, except the front-panel holes are at 2" (5 cm) and 3-¾" (9.4 cm) up from the bottom. Drill, whittle, and glue.

7. A chair is usually a trapezoid, which means that the rungs connecting the front and back panels are not perpendicular.

Materials: 2 panels just made and 4 more rungs, about 3-½" (8.9 cm) long.

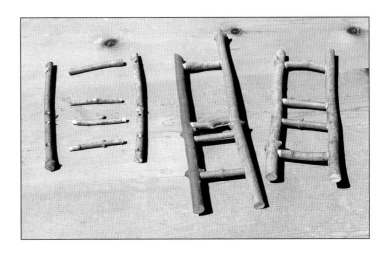

Put marks on the front of the back panel at 2-½" (6.4 cm) and just above the seat rungs at 3-¾" (9.4 cm). Drill these two holes at a tipped out angle.

8. Put marks on the inside of the front panel at 2 ½" (6.4 cm) and just above the seat rungs at 4" (10 cm). Drill these two holes at a tipped in angle. Whittle your rungs to fit and assemble the chair. Any changes? If not, glue all the pieces and strap the chair for 30 minutes with a clamp or a tourniquet made with a piece of rope.

9. Lightly sand the chair and scrape off any excess glue. Wipe an oily rag over the sanded chair and dry off any excess oil. Fashion a seat for the chair from rags, weeds, moss, or string.

10. Admire your work. Things to consider: you can make your chair into a bed by using longer side rungs. These are exactly the same steps for building bigger chairs and the same techniques for making any other kind of rustic furniture. Borrow your designs from existing furniture and copy it in sticks. If you don't believe me, try the next chair; it's like the ones I first built for my daughters.

# Projects With Natural Forms

## RUSTIC CHILD'S CHAIR
### Materials

2 sticks for back posts, 22" (55.9 cm) long
   and 1" (2.5 cm) in diameter

4 sticks for back rungs, 10-¼" (26 cm) long
   and ¾" (1.9 cm) in diameter

2 sticks for front posts, 13" (33 cm) long
   and 1" (2.5 cm) in diameter

2 sticks for front rungs, 13-½" (33.8 cm) long
   and ¾" (1.9 cm) in diameter

4 sticks for side rungs, 8-¾" (21.9 cm) long
   and 1" (2.5 cm) in diameter

2 sticks for arms, 12" (30 cm) long and
   1" (2.5 cm) in diameter

2 slender forked twigs about 11" (27.5 cm)
   long and ½" (1.3 cm)  in diameter

scrap stick

scrap twig

## Tools and Supplies

vise

pencil

electric drill with ⅝" (1.5 cm) and
   ⅜" (1.0 cm) drill bits

sharp carving knife

wood glue

twine

mallet

50' (15 m) of cloth seating tape,
   ⅝" (1.5 cm) wide

small tacks

## Procedure

Note: This chair uses mortise-and-tenon joinery. None of the tenons should be tapered and they should fit tightly in the ⅝" (1.5 cm) holes drilled for them.

1. Secure one of the back posts in a vise and mark along the stick in a straight line at points 4", 8", 11", and 21" (10.2 cm, 20.3 cm, 27.9 cm, and 53 cm) from the bottom end. Drill a ⅝" (1.5 cm) hole ⅝" (1.5 cm) deep at each mark. Repeat with the other back post.

2. Whittle tenons ⅝" (1.5 cm) long and ⅝" (1.5 cm) in diameter on both ends of the four back rungs.

3. When all the tenons fit tightly, glue them into the holes on the two back posts to fashion the ladderlike structure that will form the back of the chair. Make a tourniquet clamp by wrapping a piece of twine several times around the two posts, tying the ends together, and tightening it with a stick used as a winder (see Figure 1).

4. Secure one of the front posts in a vise and mark along the stick in a straight line at points 3" (7.6 cm) and 8" (20.3 cm) from the bottom. Drill ⅝"-holes (1.5 cm), ⅝" (1.5 cm) deep at each mark. Repeat with the other front post.

5. Whittle tenons ⅝" (1.5 cm) long and ⅝" (1.5 cm) in diameter on both ends of the two front rungs.

6. When all the tenons fit tightly, glue them into the holes on the two front posts. Secure with a tourniquet clamp and set aside to dry.

7. When the joints have dried, place the back assembly on a work table. Mark on the front

side of each post at 4-½" (11.4 cm) and 8-½" (21.4 cm) from the bottom and drill ⅝"-holes (1.5 cm), ⅝" (1.5 cm) deep. Mark the front assembly on the back side of each post at 4" (10.2 cm) and 9" (22.9 cm) from the bottom and drill ⅝"-holes (1.5 cm), ⅝" (1.5 cm) deep.

8. Whittle tenons ⅝" (1.5 cm) long and ⅝" (1.5 cm) in diameter on both ends of the four side rungs. When all the tenons fit tightly, glue the chair together and secure with tourniquet clamps in both directions.

9. Whittle tenons ⅝" (1.5 cm) long and ⅝" (1.5 cm) in diameter on one end of each arm. If you are lucky, you may be able to find a stick with a natural crook that will fit around a front post.

10. Position one of the arms in a manner you like, with the tenon butting against the chair back. Mark where the tenon should go and drill a ⅝"-hole (1.5 cm), ⅝" (1.5 cm) deep at the proper angle. Fit your tenon in the hole, trimming if necessary. Lay the other end of the arm against the outside of the front post at the desired position and drill a ⅜" (1.0 cm) hole through the arm and about ½" (1.3 cm) into the post.

11. Glue the arm tenon into its hole on the back post. Whittle a peg 2" (5 cm) long and ⅜" (1.0 cm) in diameter from a piece of twig. Apply a dab of glue to the peg and use the mallet to drive the peg through the arm until it sticks out from the other side. Put a dab of glue in the

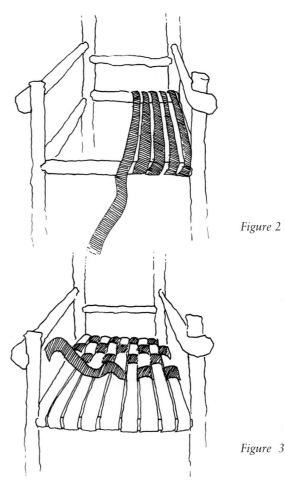

*Figure 2*

*Figure 3*

hole on the side of the arm and front post. Insert the protruding peg into the hole and drive it home. Trim the peg flush with the arm.

11. To attach the other arm, repeat Steps 10 and 11.

12. The two forked twigs add visual interest to the back of the chair. Place them in position and then mark and drill holes in the back to accommodate the twig ends; glue the twigs in place.

13. Now you are ready to weave the seat. Tack one end of your seating material to the rear underside of the seat frame. Bring the other end up and outside the rail and wrap it around and around across the front and back rails until the surface is full, then tack it under the frame (see Figure 2). This is the seating warp. Tack the end of the weft material to the underside center of the rear seat rail. Bring it under the first row, over the second, under the third and so on to the side rail. Bring your material up and over the side rail and weave the top in the same manner (see Figure 3). Continue back across the bottom warp, this time weaving over the first row, under the second, and so on. Continue weaving until the seat is fully covered. Tack the end of the material to the bottom.

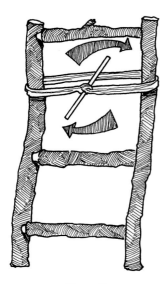

*Figure 1*

# Projects With Natural Forms

### DONNA'S HEADBOARD

Donna Rawson had never built any furniture, rustic or otherwise, when she came to a summer workshop a few years ago. Her plan was to make a chair, a headboard, and a few bedside tables. She did it all. Here's the headboard as it looks now.

And here's how it started. It represents a day's work... for a woman three months pregnant.

A frame was quickly and simply constructed from 2" (5 cm) maple saplings. There were two uprights, each 45" (114 cm) tall, and three cross pieces, each 84" (2.1 m) long. The rails were screwed in with 3" (7.6 cm) deck screws, first predrilled, then countersunk into the posts. There was an 80" (2 m) distance

between the posts...exactly the width of a king-size mattress. (This frame wiggled and racked a bit, so diagonals were added later.)

With this as the empty canvas, Donna, who is a painter, began to select and arrange the branches to fill in the frame.

After moving across a few states and in and out of a few homes, the headboard came to rest here, and was mounted 12" (30 cm) off the floor on 2' by 4' (60 x 120 cm) spacers that had been lag-screwed into the wall.

Donna and her family enjoy the woodsy look of the bed, and decorate it to mirror the changing seasons.

*This page: Donna Rawson creating her rustic headboard*

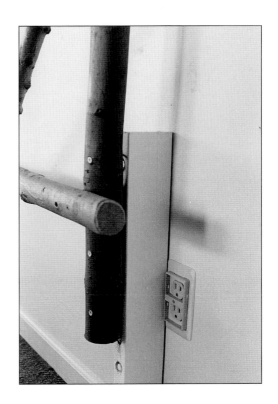

# Resources: People, Materials, Tools, Books, and Topic Information

This book has introduced the reader to many different rhythms of rustic work. These are almost all based on the overlapping rhythms of nature: the work day, the night; quiet, activity; large, small; straight, curved; movement, stillness; planned, unexpected; this list continues.

This final section is a list of "resources".. actually it's like a lunch box... a little something to keep you going on your journey: people to contact, where to get your tools, how high a table really is, and rustic places to visit and stay. It's the next stuff to make your experiences out of. This farewell list can help you find and enjoy your own rhythms in the rustic world... You may be a worker bee who likes tools; or a butterfly who enjoys visiting the lodges and museums; a grasshopper taking workshops... Whatever your interest in this field, here are the places to start to get more involved.

*Above and right: Big Cedar Lodge, Ridgedale, MO*

# APPENDIX I:
# CONTEMPORARY MAKERS OF RUSTIC FURNITURE

## Northeast

Jean Armstrong
PO Box 607
Tupper Lake, NY 12986
518-359-9983

Jack Beck
69 Gary Drive
Brockport, NY 14420
716-637-5014

Barney Bellinger
171 Paradise Point
Mayfield, NY 12117
518-661-6563

Ted Box
18 N Summer Street
Edgartown, MA 11547
508-627-3121

Lillian Dodson
133 Crooked Hill Road
Huntington, NY 11743
516-427-2950

Jerry/Jessica Farrell
Box 255
Sidney Center, NY 13839
607-369-4916

Barry Gregson
Charlie Hill Road
RR Box 88
Schroon Lake, NY 12870
518-532-9384

Bobby Hansson
2068 Tome Highway
Port Deposit, MD 21904
410-658-3959

Timothy Hayes
RR1 Box 168
Brattleboro, VT 05301
802-254-8448

Daniel Mack
14 Welling Avenue
Warwick, NY 10990
914-986-7293

Nick Nickerson
PO Box 618
Copake, NY 12516
518-329-1664

Tom Phillips
Star Rt 2
Tupper Lake, NY 12986
518-359-9648

*William McCardle*

Dave Robinson
515 Tuxford Court
Trenton, NJ 08638
609-737-8996

David H.G. Rogers
Box 486
Glenwood Landing, NY
11547
516-759-6422

James Roth
PO Box 15
Warren, VT 05764
802-496-6859

Dennis Smith
RFD 3
Malone, NY 12953

Judd Spencer Weisberg
Rt 42 Box 177
Lexington, NY 12452
518-989-6583

## Midwest

Greg Adams
702 Main Street Box 745
Lapel, IN 46051
317-534-3009

Greg Boik
PO Box 11
Harrisville, MI 48740

Andy Brown
PO Box 466
Lakeside, MI 49116
616-469-4220

Bill Brown
Rt 1 Box 62
Park Rapids, MN 56470
218-732-3866

Bill Carlson
913 S. Mallard Drive
Palatine, IL 60067
708-776-9327

# Resources: People, Materials, Tools, Books, and Topic Information

Tim/Gloria Clark
Willow Shop
PO Box 412
Lawton, MI 49065
616-624-7268

Gary Dannels
307 Kilbourn
Beacon, IA
515-673-6210

Tor Faegere
1600 Ashland
Evanston, IL 60201
708-869-1969

Dan Haataja
Rt 2 Box 220
Menahga, MN 56464

Bud Hanzlick
Box 323
Belleville, KS 66935
913-527-2427

Larry Hawkins
10476 Bassett
Livonia, MI 48150
313-462-4914

K.L. Holt
3729 N Ravenswood
Chicago IL 60613
312-549-7154

Beth Humphreys
13084 Groman
New Buffalo, MI 49117
708-858-1306

Liz Hunt
Box 218176
Columbus, OH 43221
614-459-1551

Rodney Leesbury
Rt 2 Box 133
Nevis, MN 56467

*Daniel Mack*

Mike Miller
8290 N 375
E Lebanon, IN 46052
317-325-4005

Cliff Monteith
PO Box 165
Lake Ann, MI 49650
616-275-6560

Ken Peter
Timbridge Lumber
3703 Hautala Road
Cloquet, NM 55720
218-879-6665

**West**

Jim Barnaby
PO Box 203
Bozeman, MT 59715
406-587-3585

Diane Cole
10 Cloninger Lane
Bozeman MT 59715
406-586-3746

Diane/Indy Corson
13750 Kelly Canyon
Bozeman, MT 59715
406-587-0672

*Michael Armstrong*

Jim Dobbie
1450 Tucker Road
Hood River, OR 97031
503-387-2952

Michael Emmons
Partington Ridge
Big Sur, CA 93920
408-667-2133

Jimm Gibbs
42107 NE Goodnight Road
LA Center, WA 98629
360-225-3144

Kay Kammerzell
2711 30th Street
Bellingham, WA 98225
360-676-7171

Don C. King
HC67 Box 2079
Challis, ID 83226
(208) 838-2449

Jake Lemon
PO Box 2404
Sun Valley, ID 83353
208-788-3004

J. Mike Patrick
2811 Big Horn Avenue
Cody, WY 82414
307-587-2839

Steve Weih
Casper Mountain
Rt 46
Casper, WY 82601
307-577-2476

### West Coast/Northwest

California Twig Furniture
PO Box 1337
Lake Elsinore, CA 92531
909-674-6660

*James Roth*

# Resources: People, Materials, Tools, Books, and Topic Information

Mark/Cynthia Lee
PO Box 1454
Crescent City, CA 95531
707-464-5901

Brent McGregor
Box 1477
Sisters, OR 97759
541-549-1322

Susan Parish
2898 Glasscock
Oakland, CA 94601
510-261-0353

David Lee Sullenger
135 Stanoaks Drive
Laguna Beach, CA 92651
714-494-3509

Micki Voisard
999 Conn Valley Road
St. Helena, CA 94574
707-963-8364

Chris Windsor
14037 SE 128th Street
Renton, WA 98059
206-228-2754

## South

Don Burdick
1230 NW 55th St.
Gainesville, FL
904-378-7625

Thomas Lynch
PO Box 114
Rock Cave, WV 26234
304-924-5852

William McCardle
7628 CR 381
Tyler, TX 75708
903-593-5932

Dan Quinn
103 Wilson Creek Road
Cullowhee, NC 28723
704-293-7155

Dwayne Thompson
Rt 2 Box 2117
Clayton, GA 30525
706-782-5164

Hutch Traver
15132 Creedmoor Road
Wake Forest, NC 27587
919-528-0458

Dan Wrinkle
HC 38 Box 340
Green Springs Road
Winchester, VA 22601

## International

G. Clements
10 Palmer Street
Rocky Point 2259 NSW
Australia

Brian Cowell
Site G C-5
RR1 70 Mile House BC
Canada V0K2K0

Norma Horte
RR1 Box 2
Grande Prarie Alberta
Canada T8V2Z8

Ted Ingham
225 E. 1st Street
North Vancouver, BC
Canada VTL184
604-988-8845

Devone Johnston
Site 23
Box 10 RR 8
Calgary, AB
Canada T2J2T9
403-931-3888

Ian Jonson
8 Tainui Tce
Wellington, NZ
4-304-3400

Richard Lee
Riverside Cottage
22 Prout Bridge Beamiister
Dorset DT83AY UK
FAX 0308 863719

*Twin Farms, Barnard, VT*

## Materials
Birch bark
Good Wood
Rt. 2 Box 447A
Bethel, VT 05032

## Seating Supplies and Information*
The Caning Shop
926 Gilman Street
Berkeley, CA 94710
514-527-5010

Connecticut Cane and Reed
PO Box 762B
Manchester, CT 06040
203-646-6586

Hancock Shaker Village
PO Box 898
Pittsfield, MA 01202
413-443-0188

H.H. Perkins Company
10 South Bradley Road
Woodbridge, CT 06525
203-389-9501

Plymouth Reed & Cane
1200 W Ann Arbor Road
Plymouth, MI 48170
313-455-2150

Shaker Workshops
PO Box 1028
Concord, MA 01742
617-646-8985

Shakertown at Pleasant Hill, Inc.
3500 Lexington Road
Harodsburg, KY 40330
606-734-5411

Sturges Manufacturing
Box 55
Utica, NY (wholesale quantities only)
315-732-6159

*Adirondack Museum, Blue Mountain Lake, NY*

The Unfinished Universe
525 W. Short Street
Lexington, KY 40507
606-252-3289

*(video/instruction books are available from most suppliers)

## New Tools/Supplies/ Finishes General
American Machine and Tool Company
PO Box 70
Royersford, PA 19468
610-948-0400

Bridge City Tool Works
1104 NE 28th Avenue
Portland, OR 97232
503-282-6997

Garrett-Wade
161 Avenue of Americas
New York, NY 10013
212-807-1155

Hartville Tool Value
940 West Maple Street
Hartville, OH 44632
216-877-3631

Smoky Mountain Knife Works
PO Box 4430
Sevierville, TN 37864
615-453-5871

Van Dyke's Suppliers
PO Box 278
Woonsocket, SD 57385
605-796-4425

Woodcraft Supply Corp.
210 Wood County Industrial Park
Parkersburg, WV 26102
304-428-4866

The Woodworkers Store
21801 Industrial Blvd.
Rogers, MN 55374
612-428-3200

Woodworkers Supply
1108 North Glenn Road
Casper, WY 82601
307-237-5354

# Resources: People, Materials, Tools, Books, and Topic Information

## Specialized Tools
### Cutters, knives, etc.
Brian Boggs
114 Elm Street
Berea, KY 40403
606-986-9188

Country Workshops
90 Mill Creek Road
Marshall, NC 28753

Tom Phillips
Star RT 2
Tupper Lake, NY 12986
518-359-9648

### Electric Tenon Cutters
Bignell Machine Company
516 7th Street., NE
Grand Rapids, MI 49504
616-458-2233

Morris Wood Tool Company
PO Box 249
Morristown, TN 37815-0249
615-586-0110

### Clippers and Pruners
American Standard
Company
157 Water Street
Southington, CT 06489
203-628-9643

Dorothy Biddle Service
HC 01 Box 900
Greeley, PA 18425

### Safe Finishes
Livos Finishes/Eco
Design Company
1365 Rufina Circle
Santa Fe, NM 87502
505-438-3448

### Used Tools
Classified Exchange for the
Woodworking Industry
PO Box 34908
Memphis, TN 38184
901-372-8280

## Antique Tools
Early American Industries
Association
PO Box 2128
ESP Station
Albany, NY 12220

Fine Tool Journal
PO Box 4001
Pittsford, VT 05763
800-248-8114

### Sampling of Antique Tool Dealers
### Antiques and Tools
Scott's Corners
Rt 124
Pound Ridge, NY 10576
914-764-0015

Falcon-Wood
RFD 1 Box 176
Sheffield, MA 02157
413-229-7747

Fromer's Antiques
Box 224
New Market, MD 21774
301-831-6712

Greenbrier Antiques
351 N Dancer Road
Dexter, MI 48130
313-475-2961

William Gustafson Antiques
Rt 22
Austerlitz, NY 12017
800-542-0867

David Kingston
4727 9th Avenue
Seattle, WA 98105
206-632-1067

Linders Antiques
6205 Heise Road
Clarence Center, NY 14032
716-741-3449

Ludwig's Scattered Treasures
Glenside Avenue
Glenside, PA 19038
215-887-0512

The Mechanick's Workbench
PO Box 668
Marion, MA 02738
508-748-1680

An Old Saw
Dennis Newman
Jackson, NJ
908-367-4633

The Tool Shop
1-3 Eagle Street
Ipswich, Sflk IP4 1JA
England

Two Chiselers
1864 Glen Moor Drive
Lakewood, CO
303-232-1932

Vintage Tool House
PO Box 855
Suffern, NY 10901
914-352-1347

Ye Olde Tool Shoppe
Charlottesville, VA

*Rustic furniture workshop at Museum Village, Monroe, NY*

## APPENDIX III: TOPICAL BOOKS AND MAGAZINES

Alexander, John. *How to Build a Chair From a Tree.* Newtown: Taunton Press, 1981.

Brown, John. *Welsh Stick Chairs.* Fishguard, Wales: Abercastle Publications, 1990 (and) Fresno, CA: Linden Publishing.

Gilborn, Craig. *Adirondack Furniture and the Rustic Tradition.* New York: Harry N. Abrams, 1987.

Kaiser, Harvey. *Great Camps of the Adirondacks.* David R. Godine: 1982.

Kylloe, Ralph. *Rustic Traditions.* Gibbs Smith, 1993.

Langsner, Drew. *Green Woodworking.* Asheville: Lark, 1995.

Mack, Daniel. *Making Rustic Furniture.* New York: Sterling/Lark, 1992.

**Books Available From**
Chester Book Company
4 Maple Street
Chester, CT 06412
800-858-8515

Country Workshops
90 Mill Creek Road
Marshall, NC 28753

EAIA Books
PO Box 2128 ESP Station
Albany, NY 12220

Lark Books
50 College Street
Asheville, NC 28801
800-284-3388

The Tool Chest
45 Emerson Plaza East
Emerson, NJ 07630
800-617-TOOLS

**General Interest Books**
Petrides, George. *A Field Guide to Trees and Shrubs, The Peterson Field Guide Series.* New York: Peterson, 1972.

Sutton, Myron and Ann. *Eastern Forests, Audubon Society Nature Guides.* New York: Alfred Knopf, 1985.

**Magazines**
*American Craft*
P.O. Box 3000
Denville, NJ 07834

*The Crafts Report*
700 Orange Street
Box 1992
Wilmington, DE 19899
302-656-2209

*Wood*
Locust at 17th
Des Moines, IA 50336
800-374-9663

*Woodshop News*
Pratt Street
Essex, CT 06426
203-767-8227

# Resources: People, Materials, Tools, Books, and Topic Information

## APPENDIX IV: RUSTIC ACTIVITIES AND SIGHTS

### Classes in Rustic and Traditional Woodworking/Crafts

John C. Campbell Folk School
Rt 1 Box 14 A
Brasstown, NC 28902
704-837-2775

Center for Furniture Craftmanship
125 West Meadow Road
W. Rockport, ME 04841
207-236-4737

Country Workshops
90 Mill Creek Road
Marshall, NC 28753

Daniel Mack
Rustic Furnishings
14 Welling Avenue
Warwick, NY 10990
914-986-7293

Tom Phillips
Star Rt 2
Tupper Lake, NY 12986
518-359-9648

Warwick Country Workshops
1 East Ridge Road
Warwick, NY 10990
914-986-6636

### Museums with Rustic Furniture

Adirondack Museum
PO Box 99
Blue Mountain Lake, NY 12812
518-353-7311

Buffalo Bill Museum
720 Sheridan Avenue
Cody, WY 82414
307-587-4771

Driftwood Provincial Park
Stonecliff, Ontario
Canada KOJ2KO
613-586-2553

Garden of Eden
2nd and Kansas
Lucas KS 67648
913-525-6395

Henry Ford Museum
20900 Oakwood Blvd.
Dearborn, MI 48121
313-271-1620

Shelburne Museum
PO Box 10, Route 7
Shelburne, VT 05482
802-985-3344

Shrine of the Pines
Rt 3 Box 3262
Baldwin, MI 49304
616-745-7892

Western Heritage Center
2822 Montana Avenue
Billings, MT 59101
406-256-6809

### Lodges with a Rustic Style

Big Cedar Lodge
612 Devil's Pool Road
Ridgedale, MO 65739
417-335-2777

Lake Placid Lodge
White Face Inn Road
PO Box 550
Lake Placid, NY 12946
518-523-2700

Mohonk Mountain House
Lake Mohonk
New Paltz, NY 12561
914-255-1000

The Point
HCR1 Box 65
Saranac Lake, NY 12983
518-891-5674

Post Ranch Inn
PO Box 219
Big Sur, CA 93920
408-667-2200

*Students at rustic course*

Camp Sagamore
Sagamore Road
PO Box 146
Raquette Lake, NY 13436
315-354-5311

The Swag
Rt 2 Box 280-A
Waynesville, NC 28786
704-926-0430

Timberline Lodge
Mt. Hood National Forest
Mt. Hood, OR 97028
503-272-3311

Twin Farms
PO Box 115
Barnard, VT 05031
802-234-9999

Whispering Maples B&B
Box 382
Becket, MA 01223
413-623-2392

## National and Urban Parks

National Parks in the United States embrace a "harmony with the landscape" that is reflected in the buildings constructed in the 1920s. Visits to Yosemite, Bryce, Zion, Mount Hood, and the Grand Canyon yield a grand interpretative vision of the rustic spirit. Similarly many urban parks, notably Central Park and Brooklyn's Prospect Park, have old or rebuilt rustic structures.

## Annual Rustic Events

Adirondack Antiques Show
Adirondack Museum
PO Box 99
Blue Mountain Lake, NY 12812
518-352-7311 or 352-7312
September

Rustic Makers Day
Adirondack Museum
PO Box 99
Blue Mountain Lake, NY 12812
518-352-7311 or 352-7312
September

Western Design Conference
1108 14th Street, #105
Cody, WY 82414
307-587-5898
September

## Dealers of Rustic Furniture

Boney Woods
Gallery PO Box 31
Barnet, VT 05821
802-633-4031

Bert Savage
Larch Lodge
Center Stafford, NH 03815
603-269-7411

*Twin Farms, Barnard, VT*

## APPENDIX V: GENERAL FURNITURE DIMENSIONS

Measurements are like laws: They are an agreed upon standard devised from watching how people behave. One of the enjoyments of rustic work is that people don't expect this furniture to behave like other furniture, so the builder has an opportunity to gently or dramatically surprise the user with something quite novel in its dimensions or quite accommodating in its comfort. Here are some general dimensions for the most common forms of furniture— chairs, tables, and beds. When in doubt, refer to your local piece of comfortable furniture.

### Chairs
A chair is as average as a body... each body has different aches and pains; it's always changing a bit here and there; it squirms around in a chair. Each culture has different guidelines for what's appropriate or comfortable... so what was that question again?

One very common rustic event is the chair that got away...a chair that has unusually generous proportions and resists passing through doorways. These guidelines will not protect you from the Big Chair, but they will help you figure out something for other chairs and tables and beds. Because almost all rustic furniture is custom, these dimensions will and should vary.

| Chairs | Seat ht | Seat dth OD | Seat wdth front OD | Back Post Ht |
|---|---|---|---|---|
| Dining, arm | 18" | 16"-20" | 20"-25" | 36"-47" |
| Dining, side | 18" | 16"-20" | 18"-20" | 36"-47" |
| Kitchen | 17"-18" | 14"-16" | 14"-16" | 30"-36" |
| Club chair with cushion | 16"-17" | 24"-26" | 25"-28" | 36"-47" |
| Ottoman | 17" | 17" | 17" | |
| Bar stool | 24"-28" | 16"-18" | 16"-18" | 32"-42" |

## Tables

Tables are somewhat more standard than chairs, although they should cooperate with the needs of the user and the surrounding furniture. Key decisions for dining tables involve the distance to set back the legs from the ends and sides to give stability yet allow for easy sitting on the ends and sides. Each person should have 24 inches of tabletop and the apron should be 24 inches from the floor. Another variable is the finished height from the floor; this varies from 29 to 31 inches. Often rustic tables include roots and twisted branches that eat up available space and diminish the utility of the table.

*Dining Tables:  Sample size and seating capacity*

| Diameter | Seating | | L" x W" | Seating |
|---|---|---|---|---|
| 60" round | 7–8 people | | 60 x 60 | 8–12 people |
| 48" round | 5–6 people | | 54 x 54 | 6–8 people |
| 42" round | 4–5 people | | 48 x 48 | 6–8 people |
| | | | 42 x 42 | 4 people |
| | | | 36 x 36 | 4 people |

| L" x W" | Seating |
|---|---|
| 120 x 48 | 11–-12 people |
| 108 x 48 | 8–10 people |
| 84 x 42 | 8 people |
| 72 x 36 | 6 people |
| 60 x 30 | 4 people |

| *Other Tables* | Height | Length | Width |
|---|---|---|---|
| Coffee | 14"-18" | min 24" | min 20" |
| Sofa Table | 26"-31" | min 60" | 12"-18" |
| Side Table | 19"-21" | 24" | 8" |
| Nightstand | 21"-27" | min 12" | min 12" |
| Desk | 29"-30" | min 54" | min 24" |

## Beds

Beds are pretty regular because there are standards for mattresses and box springs, but there are various and changing tastes in how high off the floor the mattress should be. The average headboard is about 44 inches tall and mattresses are about 23 inches off the floor. Rustic beds are often quite a bit taller. I make my "regular" headboard 54 inches tall with a short 32-inch footboard. Usually I leave about an inch around the box springs and mattress. Watch out for rustic elements which bow into the area needed for the box springs and mattresses.

Here are the Mattress Industry Standards for width and length of mattresses and box springs.

| *Beds* | Mattress | Box Springs |
|---|---|---|
| Twin | 38" x 74.5" | 37.5" x 74" |
| Twin Long | 38" x 79.5" | 37.5" x 79" |
| Double | 53" x 74.5" | 52.5" x 74" |
| Double long | 53" x 79.5" | 52.5" x 79" |
| Queen | 60" x 79.5" | 59.5" x 79" |
| King | 76" x 79.5" | 37.5" (2) x 79" |
| California King | 72" x 83.5" | 35.5" (2) x 83" |

# Index

*Windle Dills in workshop, 1993*

## INDEX